Studies in
Metaphysical Poetry

Studies in
Metaphysical Poetry

THEODORE SPENCER

and

MARK VAN DOREN

TWO ESSAYS

AND A BIBLIOGRAPHY

KENNIKAT PRESS, INC./PORT WASHINGTON, N.Y.

STUDIES IN METAPHYSICAL POETRY

Copyright 1939 Columbia University Press
This edition published in 1964 by KENNIKAT PRESS

Library of Congress Catalog Card No: 64-15543

Manufactured in the United States of America

Preface

THE Seventeenth Century Section of the Modern Language Association of America, for the annual meeting of the Association at Chicago in 1937, invited Mr. Van Doren and me to present a survey and analysis of the scholarly and critical work which has been done on metaphysical poetry during the past twenty-five years. Our papers, together with the bibliography which was the basis of our discussion, form the present volume.

The bibliography attempts to give a complete list (though only the most important book reviews are included) of all scholarly and critical writing on metaphysical poetry which has appeared in print from the publication of Grierson's edition of Donne in 1912 until May 1, 1938.

T. S.

ELIOT HOUSE
CAMBRIDGE, MASS.
SEPTEMBER, 1938.

Contents

Recent Scholarship in Metaphysical Poetry

❧

By THEODORE SPENCER

THE accompanying bibliography of scholarship and criticism concerning metaphysical poetry during the last twenty-five years indicates very clearly how much attention has recently been paid to the subject and how important a place it has had in the literary interests of our time. The list of titles is, I believe, at least twice as long as a similar list would be for the whole nineteenth century. And it reflects, not merely an antiquarian curiosity, but a real excitement about a type of poetry which recent poets have much admired, and which was the expression of a generation faced by many problems similar to our own.

In briefly surveying the material which this bibliography contains it will not be necessary, of course, to give a detailed account of all the scholarly work included. What I shall try to do is to describe the main scholarly achievements in the field and the tendencies which they represent; to mention certain work that is at present under way and to point out what appear to be further desiderata; and, finally, to come to some conclusions about the significance of this twenty-five years' work for the history of literary and scholarly opinion.

The first difficulty that presents itself when such a survey is attempted is the difficulty of what to call "criticism" and what to call "scholarship." In this

particular field and in this particular period, the two
are very closely related. Professor Grierson's definitive
edition of Donne in 1912, for example, is primarily a
work of scholarship, yet the fact that it was undertaken
at all represents a critical interest of which it was at
the time a culmination and for which it has since been
a stimulus. The critical essays, as well as the poetic
practice, of Mr. T. S. Eliot have doubtless hastened
scholarly investigation of the poets he has reinter-
preted, and the scholarly investigation has quickened
fresh critical discrimination. Nevertheless, in spite of
these and similar difficulties, the distinction between
scholarship and criticism is useful to make, and hence
I shall limit myself in this discussion to three types of
work: (1) editions based on careful collations of texts,
(2) exhaustive monographs, (3) articles concerned
with factual discoveries.

At the beginning of the period under survey, in
1912, most of the metaphysical poets needed careful
re-editing. There were, to be sure, various nineteenth-
century reprints, and, for those who lived near large
libraries, whose ears were deaf to the niceties of prose
rhythm, and whose eyes were blind to textual inac-
curacies, there was always the work of the indefati-
gable and polysyllabic Grosart. In addition the Muses'
Library had printed editions of Donne, Crashaw, and
others, but the texts were by no means invariably
critical, and they were not provided with the desir-
able scholarly apparatus.

Grierson's edition of Donne in 1912 set the high
standard to which subsequent editors have been
obliged to conform. His careful examination of the

manuscripts, his learned and illuminating footnotes, his discriminating criticism made his two volumes a model, and the re-examination of the sources by John Hayward—in preparation of his 1929 Nonesuch edition of Donne—only confirmed Sir Herbert's text.

The number of editions of metaphysical poets which followed Grierson is a good indication of the popularity of those poets during the following twenty-five years. The poems of Henry King have been edited by Lawrence Mason (Yale University Press, 1914), by George Saintsbury (*Minor Poets of the Caroline Period*, Oxford, 1921, Vol. III), and by John Sparrow (Nonesuch, 1925). The Clarendon Press has published L. C. Martin's editions of Vaughan (1914) and of Crashaw (1927) and The Oxford Press has published H. M. Margoliouth's edition of Marvell (1927)—all three representing texts which must be taken as standard. The George Herbert Palmer edition of Herbert, first printed in 1905 (Cambridge, Mass.), was reprinted in 1916 (New York: Houghton Mifflin). Dobell's edition of Traherne was revised by Miss G. I. Wade in 1932 (London: Dobell). The Nonesuch Press of London has done much to make the metaphysical poets available in an attractive and readable form. From 1923 to 1929 they issued texts of Cowley, Donne, Marvell, Vaughan, King and Herbert. And in addition to these—omitting a large number of reprints by popular and private presses—there have been at least ten anthologies of seventeenth-century verse, in every one of which a considerable part has been concerned with metaphysical poetry. Today no lover of metaphysical poetry can complain, as he could have complained two generations ago, that the texts of his favorite poets are hard to get at. There is only one important omission; the works of Carew, as C. L. Powell pointed out as long ago as 1916,[1] need a modern editor. It is to be hoped that this task will shortly be accomplished, if it is not—unknown to the present writer—already under way.

Donne, naturally enough, has received more scholarly and critical attention during the past twenty-five years than any of the other metaphysicals. His fascinating and bewildering personality, his learned and complicated mind, the vigor and excitement of his poetry, the representative, even symbolic, character of all he did and wrote have been the subjects of a great deal of investigation, which is by no means at an end. I can perhaps best give an indication of the kind of attention which metaphysical poetry has recently received, by surveying briefly what has been written about Donne.

In the first place, certain new facts of considerable interest about his life have been discovered. The date of his birth, erroneously given by Walton as 1573, has been in all probability correctly set at between January and June of 1572.[2] The amount of his patrimony has been established, from records in the Guildhall, at about £750.[3] Mr. I. A. Shapiro has summarized Donne's connection with Thavies' Inn and

---

[1] "New Materials on Thomas Carew," *Modern Language Review*, 11: 285–297.

[2] F. P. Wilson, "Notes on the Early Life of John Donne," *Review of English Studies*, 3 (1927): 272–279.

[3] *Ibid.*

Lincoln's Inn from 1591 to 1594;[4] the date of Donne's travels, one of the most vexed points in Donne's chronology, has been set by Mr. John Sparrow as 1594–1595.[5] Perhaps the most interesting fact about Donne's life that has recently been brought to light is that he was twice a member of Parliament: once in 1601, as Egerton's secretary, when there is no record of his activities, and later in 1614, when he was a member of several committees. As Mr. Shapiro remarks, "Donne's membership of Parliament in 1614 reinforces other evidence that he was at this time making energetic efforts to obtain political preferment, and supports the conclusion that his final decision to enter the Church, made a few months after the 'Addled' Parliament was dissolved, was taken with extreme reluctance, and only because all hope of civil preferment having failed and his fortunes being now desperate, Donne saw in the Church the only means of providing for his family."[6] Further information of interest about Donne's life will unquestionably be provided in Mr. Shapiro's forthcoming edition of the letters. They are the main source for our knowledge of Donne's history between his marriage and his ordination, and Mr. Shapiro's careful examination of their chronology and their recipients is bound to throw new light on Donne's activities,

[4] "John Donne and Lincoln's Inn," *Times Literary Supplement*, 1930, Oct. 16, Oct. 23.

[5] "The Date of Donne's Travels," in Theodore Spencer, ed., *A Garland for John Donne*, Cambridge, Mass.: Harvard University Press, 1931, p. 151.

[6] I. A. Shapiro, "John Donne and Parliament," *Times Literary Supplement*, 1932, March 10.

particularly during that period in his life. Mr. Shapiro has already promised evidence, for example, which he believes will show that *Biathanatos* was written later than 1608, the date now generally assigned to it. In addition to this, Mr. John Sparrow has for some years been engaged on a complete biography—a work which, as everyone knows, is badly needed to replace the enthusiastic but hardly flawless volumes of Gosse.

About Donne's thought much has been written, much has been disputed, and something has been learnt in the past twenty-five years. The quantity of work has had both benefits and disadvantages. As Mr. Merritt Y. Hughes has pointed out in his learned and lively article, "Kidnapping Donne,"[7] a number of critics and scholars, the scholars limping behind the critics, have seen in Donne a paganism and a skepticism which is not his, but our own. They have tried to see Donne, not as a seventeenth-century figure, but as a man of our own time. This tendency, now that the peak of the enthusiasm for Donne is perhaps over, has fortunately dwindled, and we are beginning to get a truer picture of the content of Donne's mind in relation to the complicated intellectual trends which influenced it.

Here again, Sir Herbert Grierson has been a leader. The notes to his edition show the kind of learning which crammed Donne's mind—the writings of the church fathers, the scholastic philosophers, the law, contemporary science and literature. But as Sir Herbert himself pointed out,[8] one part of Donne's back-

[7] *University of California Publications in English*, 4 (1934): 61–89.
[8] In his edition of Donne's poems, Vol. 2, p. 5, n. 1.

ground—scholastic philosophy and theology—needed,
at the time of his edition, further attention. That attention students of Donne soon increasingly proceeded
to give. The first full treatment of the relation of
Donne's thought to medieval teaching was by Miss
M. P. Ramsay in her thesis for the Paris doctorate in
1917: *Les Doctrines médiévales chez Donne, le poète métaphysicien de l'Angleterre* (London: Milford). Miss Ramsay's
work was thorough and well documented, but her
conclusions have not been wholly accepted. As a
pupil of Picavet she laid great stress on the Neo-
platonic character of medieval thought, and, in not
giving what most authorities are agreed is the correct
picture of medievalism, she failed to present a true
account of its reflection in Donne's mind. As Professor
Bredvold has observed,[9] by making Donne an ex-
ponent of Plotinianism she simplified "beyond recog-
nition his complex and enigmatic personality," and
removed "from the story of his inner life that element
of dramatic uncertainty and suspense which makes his
biography so fascinating."

A further attempt at summarizing Donne's thought
was made in 1924 by Mrs. E. M. Simpson in the fifth
chapter of her *Study of the Prose Works of John Donne*
(Oxford: Clarendon, 1924). But this account, though
it is based on a wide reading in Donne's own work
and is presented clearly and comprehensively, suffers
from two faults: it accepts Miss Ramsay's conclusions
uncritically, and it studies Donne too much as an

---

[9] L. I. Bredvold, "The Religious Thought of Donne," *University
of Michigan Publications, Language and Literature*, 1 (1925): 196.

isolated figure, without sufficiently relating his views to his background and his time.

A truer picture of Donne's intellectual climate was given, in 1923 and 1925, in two articles by Professor Bredvold.[10] He analyzed Donne's early poems in relation to the naturalism and skepticism of the sixteenth century and discussed his religious thought in relation to the inherited problem of faith and reason. He pointed out that Donne's earlier thought has some similarities—in spite of great temperamental divergences—to that of Montaigne, while Donne's later emphasis on faith as opposed to reason, a corollary (or a cause) of his dependence on St. Augustine, shows certain resemblances to Pascal. Professor Bredvold's approach to the subject has led to further fruitful results. Instead of making vague and unprofitable comparisons between Donne and Browning or Donne and Blake, students of Donne have concentrated on his relation to the poetic and intellectual fashions of his own period. In 1925 Mario Praz published his excellent book on Donne and Crashaw, *Secentismo e Marinismo in Inghilterra*, in which he not only gives a clear account, one of the best that has been written, of Donne's career, but also studies his poetry in the light of Renascence poetic tradition. Here, and elsewhere, Professor Praz has emphasized the importance of that tradition to a full understanding of Donne's subject matter and style.

Donne's style has, in fact—as any one at all familiar

[10] One I have already cited. The other is "The Naturalism of Donne in Relation to Some Renaissance Traditions," *Journal of English and Germanic Philology*, 22 (1923): 471–502.

with the field is aware—received a great deal of attention during recent years. The most detailed work on the subject, as far as Donne's metrical and stanzaic technique is concerned, is the study by Pierre Legouis, *Donne the Craftsman: the Structure of the Songs and Sonnets* (1928). One can disagree on occasional points with M. Legouis, particularly with his interpretation of "The Ecstasie," and his method is sometimes mechanical, but his work has clarified our view of Donne's control of his medium. George Williamson, in *The Donne Tradition* (Cambridge, Mass.: Harvard University Press, 1930), has discussed the nature of the metaphysical style in a wider connotation: his book is one of the best examples of that union between scholarship and criticism to which I have already referred as characteristic of work in this particular field.

Miss Helen C. White, in her book, *The Metaphysical Poets: a Study in Religious Experience* (New York: Macmillan, 1936), has analyzed the character of Donne's religion and religious poetry not only against the background of the intellectual and religious climate of the early seventeenth century but also against the wider background of the relation between poetry and mysticism. Her discussion utilizes a number of recent views of seventeenth-century thought, notably those of Mr. Basil Willey in his *Seventeenth Century Background*, and describes sensitively Donne's own writing.

The most recent discussion of the content of Donne's mind is that by Professor Charles M. Coffin, *John Donne and the New Philosophy* (New York: Columbia University Press, 1937). Mr. Coffin treats for the first time in any satisfactory detail Donne's knowledge of the astronomical discoveries of his day and their effect upon his thought and expression. Now and then he mentions subjects which one wishes he had developed more fully, such as the difference in Donne's day between an Oxford and a Cambridge education, because of the Ramist controversy at Cambridge, but on the whole Mr. Coffin has given an excellent account of his subject and has clarified what has too frequently been a matter for inaccurate generalization.

Such, too briefly described, are the chief scholarly contributions to our knowledge of Donne's mind. I have omitted many shorter articles, as may be seen by a glance at the accompanying bibliography. The quantity, and the quality, of the work is impressive, and if we compare the knowledge that is available now with that which was available a generation ago, it will be clear enough how much has been accomplished.

The direction which the work has taken is also interesting, for it appears to illustrate certain national differences as well as a tendency that is widespread in contemporary American scholarship as a whole. If we survey the period, we can say, broadly speaking, that the more detailed work of editing, etc. has come from England, while the more general work, the attempt to see Donne's mental background, has come from this country. There are exceptions, of course, and the difference may be merely an accident, but I think that would be the general conclusion. It is an interesting reflection of what is happening in American scholarship in other fields than that of metaphysical poetry—the tendency to study the individual in terms of his age, to discuss literature in relation to the society and ideas of its time. Perhaps we in America, being further removed from the sources of European thought, feel a greater need for redescribing a background that to an Englishman is more immediate. Whatever the cause, it is a healthy sign of an awareness in this country of the deeper implications of scholarship.

The work on Donne that is at present under way in England would seem to bear out this divergence of national interests. Mr. I. A. Shapiro's edition of Donne's letters should appear within a year or two. Mr. John Sparrow is withholding his life of Donne until Mr. Shapiro's work is available. Mrs. E. M. Simpson's editing of Donne's minor prose works is progressing, though it has been interrupted as a result of her collaboration with her husband on his edition of Ben Jonson. All three of these works when they appear should prove invaluable to students of Donne, and after them there would seem to be only one thing left to do: to prepare a modern edition of the sermons, a large task which, so far as my knowledge goes, no one has yet begun.

That, and possibly the preparation of a Donne concordance, seem to me the chief desiderata in the study of Donne at the moment. Of course as knowledge grows, as tastes change, and we see Donne from different perspectives, a need for new interpretations will arise. No account of that rich and many-sided mind can ever be final, as no account of any important author can be final. A poem, a school of poetry, a personality, changes with each observer and becomes part of a new pattern.

But I wonder if, for our generation at least, the study of Donne has not now reached a kind of saturation point. Perhaps it has: it is a question which I think will occur to any student of recent Donne scholarship, as it has already occurred to Mr. T. S. Eliot in another connection.[11]

I have so far described chiefly the scholarly work on Donne because, as I have suggested, it is, to use one of Donne's favorite notions, a kind of microcosm of scholarship relating to metaphysical poetry in general. The interest has spread, of course, to other writers of his school, and much has been learnt as a result of the last twenty-five years' investigation. Professor Austin Warren has, in several articles, thrown light on the career of Crashaw. Abraham Cowley has twice received extended treatment. In 1931 M. Jean Loiseau published his exhaustive study in over 700 pages, *Abraham Cowley, sa vie, son œuvre* (Paris: Didier), as well as his book, *Abraham Cowley's Reputation in England* (Paris: Didier). In the same year Professor A. H. Nethercot published his *Abraham Cowley: the Muse's Hannibal* (Oxford: Clarendon); a less monumental work, but interesting and well informed. With these volumes available, it would seem that for some time to come work on Cowley need be confined only to details.

Andrew Marvell's life and work has also been treated at length. M. Pierre Legouis' volume, *André*

[11] "Donne in our Time," in Theodore Spencer, ed., *A Garland for John Donne*, Cambridge, Mass.: Harvard University Press, 1931, pp. 1 ff.

Marvell, poète, puritain, patriote, 1621–1678, which was
the model for M. Loiseau's work on Cowley, appeared
in 1928. It corrected a number of misconceptions
about Marvell's biography and gave an extended
and illuminating commentary on Marvell's career
and writings. There were, to be sure, a few slips—
such as the translation of Donne's satirical phrase
about women, "they are but mummy, possess'd," by
"ils ne sont que des mommies, possédés par le diable"
—but these were made up for by the thoroughness
of the work as a whole. The list of exhaustive monographs may be brought to an end with a mention of
Dr. Philip W. Souers' scholarly account of the life of
Katherine Philips, *The Matchless Orinda,* which was
published in 1931 (Cambridge, Mass.).

As we examine the titles in the bibliography several
facts of considerable interest stand out. Not only is
the quantity of work impressive; it also throws a good
deal of light on the critical and scholarly taste of our
time. There seem to be, for example, definite waves
of popularity as far as the individual poets are concerned, some accidental, others springing from a
deeper cause. Among the accidental causes, anniversaries have been important: the tercentenary of
Marvell's birth in 1921 was celebrated by his native
town of Hull with elaborate ceremonies, and it pro-
duced a number of literary tributes; the tercentenary
of the death of Donne ten years later accounts in part
for the great number of studies of Donne that then
appeared. Yet these anniversaries would not have
been celebrated as enthusiastically as they have been,

if there had not been a deeper sympathy between the poets of the metaphysical school and the thought of recent times than that implied by anniversaries. It has, as one looks back over the period, been a sympathy of a curious kind, based not only on similarity but on dissimilarity as well, and hence, at times, it has turned to envy and has thus led to an even stronger attraction. The poets of the seventeenth century lived, as we have lived, in a difficult and transitional age; they were aware, as we have been aware, of conflicts that more orderly periods ignore, but they had a community of reference, a generally accepted sense of values which we lack, and their conflicts were within definite limits as ours are not. That is even more important a difference, it seems to me, than the distinction, made familiar by Mr. T. S. Eliot, between their unified sensibility and our disorganized sensibility, for their unity of sensibility sprang from a fundamental unity of conviction. If their conflict was a religious conflict, the question to decide was what kind of religion to choose; they did not have to decide whether or not one could choose any religion at all. It is a paradox, but a true one, that the necessity we are in of asking more fundamental questions than theirs has made us more superficial in our thinking and expression, so that we have turned back with a kind of nostalgia to their greater capacity for intensity and force.

And in trying to find out exactly what the metaphysical poets said, the scholarship of the past twenty-five years has done much to clarify that great difference between them and ourselves. But this scholarship,

if we define the term as I tried to define it at the
beginning of this paper, has been, on the whole, a
disciple, sometimes almost a camp follower, of the
criticism. That is another interesting fact revealed by
a study of the bibliography. And it is true in other
fields, and at other times, than this. A few sensitive
minds discover the type of past literature which seems
most congenial to them and to their age;[12] the discovery, the congeniality, spreads, and scholarship fol-
lows behind, garnering and arranging. Doubtless that
is both inevitable and right: but, as far as scholarship
in metaphysical poetry is concerned, it leaves, for the
student of contemporary taste, certain questions to be
answered.

Has the amount of scholarly work now being done
on metaphysical poetry (for it shows few signs of
diminishing) become an anachronism? In a decade
like ours, when we are no longer as interested as the
past decade was in analyzing our dilemmas and our
dichotomies, should we still be turning our scholarly
attention to a race of poets whose attempts, in Dr.
Johnson's phrase, "were chiefly analytic?" Should not
our scholarship be directed to another type of poetry
more in keeping with the general tendency of our
time, the tendency which is trying to merge analysis
in synthesis, to see the individual experience, not as
an explodable and isolated phenomenon, but as part
of a larger, a more social and religious whole?

[12] For example, Rupert Brooke's enthusiasm for Donne, at about
the time of Grierson's edition, though it found little expression
in print, was an important element in the growth of Donne's
English popularity.

For pure scholarship, which tries chiefly to describe the past as accurately as possible, these questions may be, of course, irrelevant, if not exasperating. Why should the scholar bother about being contemporary? It isn't his job. Yet in a sense it *is* his job; the scholar, like everyone else in a given time, reflects that time, no matter how unconsciously. But the more conscious he is, the better, I believe, he will be as a scholar. And the more closely he will relate his scholarship to the thought and taste of his own time, the more he will illustrate that fruitful union between scholarship and criticism which, in spite of any lag that has in the past kept them apart, has been a characteristic of recent work on metaphysical poetry.

Seventeenth-Century Poets and Twentieth-Century Critics

❦

By MARK VAN DOREN

AS GOOD a proof as any that our age is psychological may be found in its criticism of certain seventeenth-century poets. Of the fact that these poets were once said—with or without respect—to be philosophical we make little mention. Our interest is not in the thoughts they had but in the way they had them; more particularly, in their good fortune as being able to have them at all. The typical procedure takes off from an assumption that the modern mind is a split thing, its several organs or faculties operative in isolation or branching with an ever-greater divergence from what was once a main stem. The critic writes the letter Y and asks us to think of ourselves as languishing at the tip of either horn; or torn between the two; or falling in fragments between them. In the seventeenth century, the dogma is, poets like other men lived at the base of the Y. The whole person lived a whole life, and if he was a poet he wrote a whole poem: something that will never be done again until we recapture our lost integrity, until our sap drains back into the sturdy root.

This has been said in a variety of ways, and with much brilliance. "The favorite phrase," says Professor Grierson on the first page of his *Milton and Wordsworth*, "is 'unified sensibility.'" Mr. Eliot in other words has been high priest to the analysis. His famous essay of 1921, "The Metaphysical Poets," a review of Professor Grierson's own anthology, is classic in this critical literature. It contains sentences from which other sentences have been derived when they have not been merely repeated. "A thought to Donne was an experience; it modified his sensibility. When a poet's mind is perfectly equipped for its work, it is constantly amalgamating disparate experience; the ordinary man's experience is chaotic, irregular, fragmentary. The latter falls in love, or reads Spinoza, and these two experiences have nothing to do with each other, or with the noise of the typewriter or the smell of cooking; in the mind of the poet these experiences are always forming new wholes. . . . The poets of the seventeenth century possessed a mechanism of sensibility which could devour any kind of experience." But "in the seventeenth century a dissociation of sensibility set in, from which we have never recovered." Whether or not Mr. Eliot had thoroughly examined the value in his mind of the words "sensibility" and "experience," and whether he meant in the latter case experience before writing a poem or experience while writing it—the experience even *of* writing it—matters less for the moment than the fact that both terms started from his page on exceedingly active careers; the first one, "sensibility," has indeed become by now a cant word in criticism. It was used without definition in Mr. George Williamson's valuable book, *The Donne Tradition*. And it provided the text for Mr. Basil Willey's *The Seventeenth Century Background*. But Mr. Willey in an interesting paragraph explains what "unified sensibility" meant to those who had it. "It meant," he says, "the capacity to live in divided and distinguished worlds, and to pass freely to and fro between one and another, to be capable of many and varied responses to experience, instead of being confined to a few stereotyped ones. . . . The distinctions were only beginning to be made which for later ages shut off poetry from science, metaphor from fact, fancy from judgment. . . . Something of the peculiar quality of the 'metaphysical' mind is due to this fact of its not being *finally committed* to any one world. Instead, it could hold them all in a loose synthesis together, yielding itself, as only a mind in free poise can, to the passion of detecting analogies and correspondences between them." The long paragraph of which this is a part and the long book of which this is the thesis are but expansions of Mr. Eliot's brief and by his own confession tentative theory. Nothing could testify more eloquently to Mr. Eliot's ability and influence as a critic.

And it is still the best explanation we have of what I with many others take to be a fact: namely, that seventeenth-century poetry is the finest English poetry there is, and that its fineness, being in some way unique, is not approached outside the century. Nor can I feel superior to the critical tradition which draws the letter Y, since I propose to draw it once more myself. My emphasis, however, will be different, and my seriousness less. A rereading of certain books in the tradition has convinced me that we have been too solemn on the subject of "the metaphysicals." Our statement of the aesthetic problems they solved has been too ponderous for plausibility, even granting that the statement took account of the great and therefore enviable ease with which they solved them.

A discussion of what once was easy and now is difficult or impossible should in itself have ease; we should not give the impression that the seventeenth-century poets staggered under a burden of art, or at any rate that the modern reader of them must stagger under a burden of analysis. They are in fact delightful and do not appear to be in the least conscious that they have work to do for us as well as for themselves. We have tended to afflict them with our nostalgia, to beg of them that they show us our way, to torture them with disclosures of our confusion. Mr. Eliot in his essay went on to cite the difficulty of living in our time, and hence the difficulty of our poetry; implying not only that the poetry of any time must be like its life, but also that the metaphysical poets might be expected to help us in our task. But their poetry is not difficult, even if their life was. And so there may be an advantage in taking them for a few minutes as lightly as I believe they took themselves.

If the procedure calls for a certain detachment and for as long a critical perspective as we possess, we shall, in addition, be free of the responsibility to take seriously a considerable amount of bad poetry. Dr. Johnson was partly right, just as we on occasion have been solemnly wrong. I have seen intolerable lines praised for no better reason than that they illustrated the mental processes of a metaphysical poet. The best is so good by any standard that we do not need to make such mistakes about the mediocre or the worst. A theory as to how an artist worked is likely to inspire us with an undue affection for those pieces which show him most clearly at work. But these are probably not his best pieces, and certainly they are not if too many tools have been left lying around. There is the further danger that we do not know his method as perfectly as we think we do; our theory may express our predicament rather than his, and indeed it can be altogether wrong.

By the term "metaphysical poet" I am afraid I mean nothing more or less than "seventeenth-century poet," my authority for this license being the habit which has grown generally upon criticism of finding the special quality of the time diffused through all its best poets. This seems to me right in the abstract, and accurate as to the seventeenth century taken everywhere at its finest.

To come now to my Y, which after all is not as novel as I may seem to have promised. The horns are serious verse and light verse—or, in the language we instinctively use, poetry and light verse. The distinction is modern, and it is unfortunate. It means that we expect too little from the writer of either thing, and get too little. We expect on the one horn wit without poetry, and on the other horn poetry without wit; in the first case we get the silly and in the second case we get the insane—or, short of that, the sentimental and the sombre. The world of poetry was better ordered when the division did not exist; when every poem was free to be both smiling and true. The greatest lyric poets of the seventeenth century were in the same breath its lightest poets. The secret may be impossible to relearn, but the fact should be stated. It is perhaps explainable by the theories which I have credited to Mr. Eliot and his followers; yet I shall use none of their polysyllables if I can help it, nor shall I darken the theme with elegies for a lost age. Much as contemporary poetry has learned from the metaphysicals, or rather from the seventeenth century at its general best, it has not learned lightness; and the fault may lie with the tone of the criticism which has accompanied and supported it—even goaded it. The contemporary poet is not allowed to forget that his art is difficult. When he himself turns critic he is likely to take a perverse pleasure in proving the art, indeed, to be impossible. He prescribes both to himself and to others a small output. The prolific poet is suspect, along with the poet who has made the tactical error of striving to make it appear that he has written with ease out of the abundance of his nature and his opportunity. The appearance of labor is not only preferred; it is praised.

Wit, of course, has always been the key word in any discussion of seventeenth-century poetry, and it will be essential to mine, since there is a necessary connection between the thing for which it stands and the lightness whereof I speak. I do not mean by lightness anything less substantial than daylight, or anything more trivial than truth—which, be it remembered, contains many mockeries, both major and minor, and is best endured by the strongest man, the man with the most nature in him—the man, shall we say, who is best-natured. The seventeenth-century poets were, as men, well-natured and strong; one can imagine that they agreed to be men first and poets afterwards. Carew's elegy for Donne praised him because he had "drawn a line of masculine expression."

The distinction is not so much between the masculine and the feminine as between the human and the literary; the hand that wrote was quite as valuable as the thing written: the poem was something to which it turned from other occupations—war and arms, reading and thinking, drinking and dressing, conversation and love. Large as the poems are, the men are still larger; they have always a reserve of nature from which further poems, and further actions, can be drawn. They do not condescend to their poems; they give them their full attention and their whole strength; but the delicacy with which they work suggests the sensitivity of powerful fingers, of experienced palms. The slighter hand may feel more immediately but it does not feel as long; its capacity to measure what it touches can be exhausted; so that what it writes will vary between the exquisite and the gross, the timorous and the atrocious.

If all this is true, is wit the word for it? Wit is a good word, but I think we must turn to humor also, since humor is the older, the more primitive thing, and closer to that nature of which these poets never fail to remind us. My point is not that they have more humor than wit, but that they do not have more wit than humor. It is their humor that keeps them men: men who like Hotspur can have their teeth set on edge by nothing so much as mincing poetry. The habit of Shakespeare's best poets—Hotspur, Mercutio, Hamlet—is to berate poetry. But for what? For pretending, as it so often does, that it is an end in itself and not simply the best talk of the best men. The poets of the seventeenth century are men talking. The assumption they make, however, when they agree to keep poetry in its place has nothing to do with wit. It is an expression of their humor—not a verbal thing at all, any more than laughter is, or a wise silence.

Humor is the life of their poetry; wit is its language.[1] To the objection that we have only the language after three hundred years the answer is obvious: we have the life. That it cannot be described does not mean that it cannot be known. Nor am I saying that the language is unimportant. It is important because it has preserved the life and because nothing else could have preserved it; and because, when these men lived, it was the means whereby their humor—their love of existence—became articulate as poetry. To claim more for their wit would be to do what they sometimes did, with the result that they ran into dryness. They seldom undervalued it and ran into sentiment; to rest in humor is to remain an animal, and they wanted to be men.

There can be humor without poetry—it exists everywhere—and there can be poetry without humor. This poetry would not have been if there had not been humor; and after humor, to give it outline and control, wit. Wit was the conscious control by which

[1] *Wit and Emotion in Some Poems of the Seventeenth Century*, a master's thesis written at Columbia University by Ivria Adlerblum (1937), is of great value for its account of the role played by wit in seventeenth-century poetic effects. It is from Miss Adlerblum that I have borrowed the notion of wit as a language—as an instrument of analysis which differentiated the several parts or perceptions of humor and then rearranged them according to the emphasis desired: an instrument, in other words, wherewith "the force of every surprise was measured."

imagery was set in the perspective of imagination; by which an idea became dramatic; by which exaggeration learned to know its limits. Not that there was no exaggeration. Neither humor nor poetry can do without it. But the seventeenth century knew best the secret of its power. That power we shall not feel unless it is permitted to go beyond what we have thought, but in that far place it must have a worthy object upon which to exercise itself. The century, for instance, was perfect in compliment. But there was nothing accidental about this. Donne or Carew or Marvell could praise his mistress beyond all bounds except the bounds of her merit—which, since meanwhile he had made it known, could actually appear to be understated. What the poems of these men ultimately say, though not in words, is that only too much praise is enough. Having gone that far, having seen that we understand, they smile and stop.

The critic's cue is obvious.

A Bibliography of Studies in Metaphysical
Poetry, 1912-1938

ૐ

By THEODORE SPENCER
With the assistance of EVELYN ORR

GENERAL STUDIES

1913

1. Spurgeon, Caroline F. E. Mysticism in English Literature. 168 pp. Cambridge: University Press.

1914

2. Jones, Rufus M. "Thomas Traherne and the Spiritual Poets of the Seventeenth Century." Spiritual Reformers in the 16th & 17th Centuries, pages 320–335. London: Macmillan.

1915

3. Heide, Anna von der. Das Naturgefühl in der englischen Dichtung im Zeitalter Milton's. 131 pp. Heidelberg: Carl Winter's Universitäts-buchhandlung.

1918

4. Quiller-Couch, Arthur. Studies in Literature, First Series. Contains lectures on Donne, Herbert and Vaughan, Traherne and Crashaw, 336 pp. Cambridge: University Press.

1919

5. Massingham, Harold J., editor. A Treasury of Seventeenth Century English Verse from the Death of Shakespeare to the Restoration. 399 pp. London: Macmillan.

6. Osmond, Percy H. Mystical Poets of the English Church. 436 pp. New York: Macmillan.

1920

7. Alden, Raymond M. "The Lyrical Conceits of the 'Metaphysical Poets' (Carew, Donne, and Cowley)." *Studies in Philology*, 17: 183–198.

8. Clough, Benjamin C. The Metaphysical Poets: John Donne and His School. Unpublished Harvard dissertation.

9. Clough, Benjamin C. "Notes on the Metaphysical Poets (Donne, Carew, Dryden, Butler.)" *Modern Language Notes*, 35: 115–117.

10. Parry, John J. "A Seventeenth Century Gallery of Poets." *Journal of English and Germanic Philology*, 19: 270–277.

1921

11. Clutton-Brock, Arthur. "George Herbert," "Andrew Marvell," "Henry Vaughan." More Essays on Books. London: Methuen; New York: Dutton.

12. Eliot, T. S. "The Metaphysical Poets." *Times Literary Supplement*, October 20, pages 669–670. (Reprinted in Homage to John Dryden, 1924) [*See* No. 21]; November 3, page 716.

13. Grierson, Herbert J. C., editor. Metaphysical Lyrics and Poems of the Seventeenth Century: Donne to Butler. With an essay. 244 pp. Oxford: Clarendon [*See* No. 26.]

14. Saintsbury, George. "The Metaphysical Poets." *Times Literary Supplement*, October 27, page 698; November 10, page 734.

15. Saintsbury, George, editor. Minor Poets of the Caroline Period. In three volumes. Volume Three: Cleveland, King, Stanley, Flatman, Whiting. 551 pp. Oxford: University Press.

16. Thompson, Elbert N. S. "Mysticism in Seventeenth Century Literature." *Studies in Philology*, 18: 170–231.

1922

17. Hodgson, Geraldine E. English Mystics. 387 pp. London: Mowbray.
18. Nethercot, A. H. "The Term 'Metaphysical Poets' before Johnson." *Modern Language Notes*, 37: 11–17.

1923

19. Gosse, Edmund. "Metaphysical Poetry." More Books on the Table. London: Heinemann.
20. Read, Herbert. "The Nature of Metaphysical Poetry." *Criterion*, 1: 246–266.

1924

21. Eliot, T. S. "The Metaphysical Poets." Homage to John Dryden. London: Leonard and Virginia Woolf. (Reprint of article in *Times Literary Supplement*, October 20, 1921.) [*See* No. 12.]
22. George, Robert E. G. Outflying Philosophy. A literary study of the religious element in the poems and letters of John Donne and in the works of Sir Thomas Browne and of Henry Vaughan the Silurist, together with an account of the interest of these writers in scholastic philosophy, in Platonism, and in Hermetic physic, with also some notes on witchcraft. By Robert Sencourt (pseudonym). 358 pp. Hildesheim: F. Borgmeyer. (London: Simpkin Marshall, 1925).
23. Nethercot, A. H. "The Reputation of the Metaphysical Poets during the Seventeenth Century." *Journal of English and Germanic Philosophy*, 23: 173–198.
24. Wells, Henry W. Poetic Imagery Illustrated from Elizabethan Literature. New York: Columbia University Press.

1925

25. Greenlaw, Edwin. "The New Science and English Literature in the Seventeenth Century." *Johns Hopkins Alumni Magazine*, 13: 331–359.

26. Grierson, Herbert J. C. "The Metaphysical Poets." The Background of English Literature. London: Chatto and Windus. (Reprint of introductory essay to Metaphysical Lyrics . . . Donne to Butler, 1921.) [*See* No. 13.]

27. Lea, Kathleen M. "Conceits." *Modern Language Review*, 20: 389–406.

28. Nethercot, A. H. "The Attitude toward Metaphysical Poetry in Neo-Classical England." *Chicago Abstracts of Theses, Literature*, 1: 395–397.

29. Nethercot, A. H. "The Reputation of the Metaphysical Poets during the Age of Johnson and the Romantic Revival." *Studies in Philology*, 22: 81–132.

30. Nethercot, A. H. "The Reputation of the Metaphysical Poets during the Age of Pope." *Philological Quarterly* 4: 161–179.

1926

31. Eliot, T. S. Lectures on Metaphysical Poetry. (The Clark Lectures, Trinity College, Cambridge.) Unpublished MS at Eliot House, Harvard University.

32. Hamilton, George R. "Wit and Beauty: a Study of Metaphysical Poetry (Donne and Francis Thompson)." *London Mercury*, 14: 606–620.

33. Lucas, F. L. Authors Dead and Living. Essays on Donne, Vaughan, Marvell. 307 pp. London: Chatto and Windus.

1927

34. Judson, A. C., editor. Seventeenth Century Lyrics. With short biographies, bibliographies, and notes. 432 pp. Chicago: University of Chicago Press.

35. Schelling, Felix. "Devotional Poetry in the Reign of Charles I." Shakespeare and Demi-Science. Philadelphia: University of Pennsylvania Press.

1928

36. Ault, Norman, editor. Seventeenth Century Lyrics. From the original texts. 535 pp. London: Longmans.
37. Beachcroft, T. O. "Mysticism as Criticism." *Symposium*, 2: 208–225.
38. Kemp, Violet A. "Mystic Utterance in Certain English Poets." *Hibbert Journal*, 26: 474–483.
39. Naylor, E. W. "Three Seventeenth Century Poet-Parsons (Thomas Traherne, George Herbert, Robert Herrick) and Music." *Proceedings of the Musical Association* (London), 54: 93–113.

1929

40. Blunden, Edmund. Nature in English Literature. 156 pp. London: Leonard and Virginia Woolf.
41. Grierson, Herbert J. C. Cross Currents in English Literature of the Seventeenth Century. (The Messenger Lectures, Cornell.) 358 pp. London: Chatto and Windus.
42. Hebel, J. W., and F. A. Patterson, assisted by C. M. Coffin. English Seventeenth Century Literature: a Brief Working Bibliography. 10 pp. New York: Columbia University Press.
43. Newbolt, Henry, editor. Devotional Poets of the Seventeenth Century. 293 pp. London: Nelson.
44. Patterson, F. A. *See* No. 42.

1930

45. Empson, William. Seven Types of Ambiguity. 325 pp. London: Chatto and Windus.
46. Nethercot, A. H. "The Reputation of Native versus Foreign 'Metaphysical Poets' in England." *Modern Language Review*, 25: 156–164.

1931

47. Howarth, R. G., editor. Minor Poets of the Seventeenth Century: Suckling, Lovelace, Carew & Herbert [of Cherbury]. 414 pp. London: Dent.

1932

48. Friederich, W. P. Spiritualismus und Sensualismus in der englischen Barocklyrik. 303 pp. Wien und Leipzig: Braumüller.
49. Sharp, R. L. The Revolt Against Metaphysical Poetry. Unpublished Harvard dissertation.
50. Williamson, George. "Mutability, Decay, and Seventeenth Century Melancholy." *Journal of English Literary History*, 2: 121–150.

1933

51. Quennell, Peter, editor. Aspects of Seventeenth Century Verse. 287 pp. London: Cape.
52. Smith, James. "On Metaphysical Poetry." *Scrutiny*, 2: 222–239.

1934

53. Bennett, Joan. Four Metaphysical Poets: Donne, Herbert, Vaughan, and Crashaw. 135 pp. Cambridge: University Press.
54. Hagedorn, Maria. Reformation und spanische Andachstliteratur, Luis de Granada in England. 165 pp. Leipzig: Tauchnitz.
55. Leishman, James B. The Metaphysical Poets: Donne, Herbert, Vaughan, Traherne. 239 pp. Oxford: Clarendon.
56. The Oxford Book of Seventeenth Century Verse. Chosen by Herbert J. C. Grierson and G. Bullough. 988 pp. Oxford: Clarendon.
57. Praz, Mario. Studi sul concettismo. 176 pp. Milan: Soc. Ed. La Cultura.

58. Rylands, G. "The Metaphysical Poets." *Cambridge Review*, 56: 46–47.

59. "Seventeenth Century Verse." *Times Literary Supplement*, November 1, pages 741–742.

60. Sharp, R. L. "The Pejorative Use of 'Metaphysical.'" *Modern Language Notes*, 49: 503–505.

61. Sharp, R. L. "Some Light on Metaphysical Obscurity and Roughness." *Studies in Philology*, 31: 497–518.

62. Smith, W. B. "What is Metaphysical Poetry?" *Sewanee Review*, 42: 261–272.

63. Willey, Basil. The Seventeenth Century Background. Studies in the Thought of the Age in Relation to Poetry and Religion. 323 pp. London: Chatto and Windus.

1935

64. Harrison, C. T. "The Ancient Atomists and English Literature of the Seventeenth Century." *Harvard Studies in Classical Philology*, 45: 1–79.

65. Leavis, F. R. "English Poetry in the Seventeenth Century." *Scrutiny*, 4: 236–256. (Reprinted in Revaluations, 1936.)

66. Nicolson, Marjorie. "The New Astronomy and English Literary Imagination." *Studies in Philology*, 32: 428–462.

67. Nicolson, Marjorie. "The Telescope and Imagination." *Modern Philology*, 32: 233–260.

68. Sharp, R. L. "Observations on Metaphysical Imagery." *Sewanee Review*, 43: 464–478.

69. Wild, Friedrich. "Zum Problem des Barocks in der englischen Dichtung." *Anglia*, 59: 414–422.

1936

70. Brinkley, Roberta F., editor. English Poetry of the Seventeenth Century. 599 pp. New York: Norton.

71. Brittin, N. H. "Emerson and the Metaphysical Poets." *American Literature*, 8: 1–21.

72. Brooks, Cleanth. "Metaphysical Poetry and the Ivory Tower." *Southern Review*, 1: 568–583.

73. Marshall, L. Birkett, editor. Rare Poems of the Seventeenth Century. 242 pp. Cambridge: University Press.

74. White, Helen C. The Metaphysical Poets: a Study in Religious Experience. 444 pp. New York: Macmillan.

1938

75. Seventeenth Century Studies Presented to Sir Herbert Grierson. Edited by John Purves. Contains essays by C. S. Lewis, "Donne and Love Poetry in The Seventeenth Century"; Joan Bennett, "The Love Poetry of John Donne. A Reply to Mr. Lewis"; Rev. F. E. Hutchinson, "George Herbert"; T. S. Eliot, "A Note on Two Odes of Cowley"; L. C. Martin, "Henry Vaughan and The Theme of Infancy." 404 pp. Oxford: Clarendon.

THOMAS CAREW

1916

76. Powell, C. L. "New Materials on Thomas Carew." *Modern Language Review*, 11: 285–297.

1927

77. Carew, Thomas. A Rapture. Limited edition. 14 pp. London: Golden Cockerell Press.

1929

78. Dodge, R. E. Neil. "The Text of the Gerusalemme Liberata in the Versions of Carew and Fairfax." *Modern Language Association Publications*, 44: 681–695.

1930

79. Bullock, Walter L. "Carew's Text of the Gerusalemme Liberata." *Modern Language Association Publications*, 45: 330–335.

1931

80. Howarth, R. G., editor. Minor Poets of the Seventeenth Century: Suckling, Lovelace, Carew & Herbert [of Cherbury]. 414 pp. London: Dent.

1933

81. Birss, J. H. "Thoreau and Thomas Carew." *Notes and Queries*, 164: 63.

JOHN CLEVELAND

1912

82. Berdan, J. M., editor. The Poems of John Cleveland. 270 pp. London: Frowde. (Reprint of 1903 edition.)

1921

83. Saintsbury, George, editor. Minor Poets of the Caroline Period. In three volumes. Volume Three: Cleveland, King, Stanley, Flatman, Whiting. 551 pp. Oxford: University Press.

1929

84. Williamson, George. "Three Thefts from Cleveland." *Modern Language Notes*, 44: 384–385.

1931

85. Gapp, S. V. "Notes on John Cleveland." *Modern Language Association Publications*, 46: 1075–1086.

1934

86. Levin, Harry. "John Cleveland and the Conceit." *Criterion*, 14: 40–53.

ABRAHAM COWLEY

1912

87. Cowley, Abraham. On Gardens: Two Essays by
Francis Bacon and Abraham Cowley. Philadelphia:
Jacobs.

1914

88. Cowley, Abraham. Essays and Selected Verse. 308 pp.
London: Scott.

1915

89. Gough, A. B., editor. Essays and Other Prose Writings. 406 pp. Oxford: Clarendon.

1916

90. Franklin, S. B. Studies in Abraham Cowley, 1633–
1915. Unpublished Harvard dissertation.

1919

91. Ellis, Havelock. "Abraham Cowley." *New Statesman*,
13: 369–371.
92. Shafer, Robert. "Abraham Cowley." The English Ode
to 1660. Princeton: University Press.

1920

93. Bellot, H. H. "Abraham Cowley, 1618–1667."
Nineteenth Century, 88: 462–466.

1921

94. Aldington, Richard. "Cowley and the French Epi-
cureans." *New Statesman*, 18: 133–134.
95. Moore-Smith, G. C. "Abraham Cowley and Lord
Falkland." *Notes and Queries*, Ser. 12, Vol. 9: pages
305–306.
96. Nethercot, A. H. "The Relation of Cowley's Pin-
darics to Pindar's Odes." *Modern Philology*, 19:
107–109.

1922

97. DeLoach, R. J. H. "Abraham Cowley and the Agricultural College." *Science*, 55: 127–128.

1923

98. Cowley, Abraham. Anacreon Done into English out of the Original Greek, by Abraham Cowley and S. B., 1683. 52 pp. London: Nonesuch.

99. Judson, A. C. "Abraham Cowley in Arcadia." *Sewanee Review*, 31: 220–226.

100. Lumby, J. Rawson, editor. The Essays of Abraham Cowley. Revised by Arthur Tilley. 143 pp. Cambridge: University Press.

101. Nethercot, A. H. "The Reputation of Abraham Cowley 1660–1800." *Modern Language Association Publications*, 38: 588–641.

1925

102. Ardagh, J. "Abraham Cowley." *Notes and Queries*, 148: 229.

1926

103. Sparrow, John, editor. The Mistress, with Other Select Poems, 1618–1677. 233 pp. London: Nonesuch.

104. "Cowley's Lyrics." *Times Literary Supplement*. November 18, pages 805–806.

105. Nethercot, A. H. "Abraham Cowley's 'Discourse Concerning Style.'" *Review of English Studies*, 2: 385–404.

1927

106. Cole, G. D. H., and M. I. Cole, editors. A Selection of Poems. (Ormond Poets.) 62 pp. London: Douglas.

107. Hewins, Elizabeth L. "Etherege and Cowley." *Times Literary Supplement*, October 13, page 715.

108. Sparrow, John. "The Text of Cowley's 'Mistress.'" *Review of English Studies*, 3: 22–27.

1928

109. Nethercot, A. H. "Abraham Cowley as Dramatist." *Review of English Studies*, 4: 1–24.
110. Nethercot, A. H. "Letters of Abraham Cowley." *Modern Language Notes*, 43: 369–375.

1929

111. Garrod, H. W. "Cowley, Johnson, and the 'Metaphysicals.'" The Profession of Poetry, and Other Lectures. Oxford: Clarendon.
112. Sparrow, John. "Cowley's 'Plantarum libri duo': a Presentation Copy." *London Mercury*, 20: 398–399.

1930

113. Jones, R. F. "Science and English Prose Style in the Third Quarter of the Seventeenth Century." *Modern Language Association Publications*, 45: 997–1009.
114. Nethercot, A. H. "Abraham Cowley's Essays." *Journal of English and Germanic Philology*, 29: 114–130.

1931

115. Grigson, G. "Gardener, Gentleman, and Poet." *Bookman* (London), 80: 19.
116. Loiseau, Jean. Abraham Cowley, sa vie, son œuvre. 715 pp. Paris: Didier.
117. Loiseau, Jean. Abraham Cowley's Reputation in England. 229 pp. Paris: Didier.
118. Nethercot, A. H. Abraham Cowley: the Muse's Hannibal. 374 pp. Oxford: University Press.
119. Nethercot, A. H. "Concerning Cowley's Prose Style." *Modern Language Association Publications*, 46: 962–967.

1932

120. Wallerstein, Ruth. "Cowley as a Man of Letters." *Transactions of the Wisconsin Academy of Sciences, Arts, and Letters*, 27: 127–140.

1934

121. Nethercot, A. H. "Milton, Jonson, and the young Cowley: with text of quatrain on Abraham Cowley the young poet laureat, by N. Oldisworth." *Modern Language Notes*, 49: 158–162.

122. Sparrow, John. "The Text of Cowley's Satire 'The Puritan and the Papist.' " *Anglia*, 58: 78–102.

123. Wiley, Autrey N. "Prologue and Epilogue to 'The Guardian.' " *Review of English Studies*, 10: 443–447.

1936

124. Krempien, Hans H. Der Stil der Davideis von Abraham Cowley im Kreise ihrer Vorläufer; ein Beitrag zur Untersuchung des 'metaphysical wit' und des Epos vor Milton. 147 pp. Hamburg: Friederichsen de Gruyter.

1937

125. Bald, R. C. "Three Metaphysical Epigrams." *Philological Quarterly*, 16: 403–405.

126. Cowley, Abraham. Essays. 138 pp. London: Nelson.

127. Walton, Geoffrey. "Abraham Cowley and the Decline of Metaphysical Poetry." *Scrutiny*, 6: 176–194.

1938

128. Eliot, T. S. "A Note on Two Odes of Cowley." Seventeenth Century Studies. Presented to Sir Herbert Grierson, pages 235-242.

RICHARD CRASHAW

1912

129. Crashaw, Richard. Quem vidistis pastores? A Hymn of the Nativity sung by the Shepherds. New York: Benziger.

130. Sharland, E. C. "Richard Crashaw and Mary Collet." *Church Quarterly Review.* 73: 358–363.

1914

131. Shepherd, R. A. Eric, editor. Religious Poems. (The Catholic Library.) 136 pp. St. Louis, Missouri: Herder.

1916

132. Martin, L. C. "Adonais: Crashaw and Shelley parallel." *Modern Language Review*, 11: 217.

1919

133. Spender, C. "The Life and Work of Richard Crashaw." *Contemporary Review*, 116: 210–215.

1922

134. Confrey, Burton. "A Note on Richard Crashaw." *Modern Language Notes*, 37: 250–251.

1923

135. Barker, F. E. "Religious Poems of Richard Crashaw." *Church Quarterly Review*, 96: 39–65.
136. Falls, Cyril. "The Divine Poet." *Nineteenth Century*, 93: 225–233. (Reprinted in The Critic's Armoury, 1924.) [*See* No. 139.]
137. Loudon, M. K. Two Mystic Poets, and Other Essays. 97 pp. Oxford: Blackwell.
138. Martin, L. C. "A Hitherto Unpublished Poem by (?) Richard Crashaw." *London Mercury*, 8: 159–166, 187, 414.

1924

139. Chalmers, Lord. "Richard Crashaw, Poet and Saint." In Memoriam Adolphus William Ward, Master of Peterhouse, 1900–1924, pages 47–67. Cambridge: University Press.

140. Falls, Cyril. "Divine Poet." The Critic's Armoury, pages 23–38. London: Cobden-Sanderson. (Reprint of article in *Nineteenth Century*, 1923). [*See* No. 135.]

1927

141. Martin, L. C. The Poems, English, Latin, and Greek, of Richard Crashaw. (Oxford English Texts.) 565 pp. Oxford: Clarendon.

1928

142. Eliot, T. S. "A Note on Richard Crashaw." For Lancelot Andrewes, pages 129–138. London: Faber and Gwyer.

143. Hutchinson, F. E. "Richard Crashaw, Poet and Saint." *Church Quarterly Review*, 106: 140–155.

144. Tholen, Wilhelm. Richard Crashaw: ein englischer Dichter und Mystiker der Barockzeit. Das neue Ufer, xlvii.

1931

145. Warren, Austin. "Crashaw and Peterhouse." *Times Literary Supplement*, August 13, page 621.

1932

146. Warren, Austin. "Crashaw and Saint Teresa." *Times Literary Supplement*, August 25, page 593.

147. Warren, Austin. "Crashaw's Residence at Peterhouse." *Times Literary Supplement*, November 3, page 815.

1933

148. Warren, Austin. "Crashaw's Paintings at Cambridge." *Modern Language Notes*, 48: 365–366.

149. Warren, Austin. "The Mysticism of Richard Crashaw." *Church Quarterly Review*, 116: 75–92. (Also in *Symposium*, 4: 135–155.)

1934

150. Beachcroft, T. O. "Crashaw and the Baroque Style." *Criterion*, 13: 407–425.

151. Bennett, Joan. Four Metaphysical Poets: Donne, Herbert, Vaughan, and Crashaw. 135 pp. Cambridge: University Press.

152. Warren, Austin. "The Reputation of Crashaw in the Seventeenth and Eighteenth Centuries." *Studies in Philology*, 31: 385–407.

153. Warren, Austin. "Crashaw's 'Epigrammata Sacra.'" *Journal of English and Germanic Philology*, 33: 233–239.

1935

154. Crashaw, Richard. Musicks Duell, from The Delights of the Muses or Other Poems Written on Severall Occasions, 1646. London: E. Walters.

155. Newdigate, B. H. "An Overlooked Poem by Richard Crashaw." *London Mercury*, 32: 265.

156. Wallerstein, Ruth. Richard Crashaw: a Study in Style and Poetic Development. 162 pp. University of Wisconsin Studies in Language and Literature, No. 37.

157. Warren, Austin. "Richard Crashaw, Catechist and Curate." *Modern Philology*, 32: 261–269.

1936

158. Warren, Austin. "Crashaw's Reputation in the Seventeenth Century." *Modern Language Association Publications*, 51: 769–785.

159. White, Helen C. The Metaphysical Poets: a Study in Religious Experience. 444 pp. New York: Macmillan.

1937

160. Barker, F. E. "Crashaw and Andrewes." *Times Literary Supplement*, August 21, page 608.

161. Colville, K. N. "Crashaw and Andrewes." *Times Literary Supplement*, August 28, page 624.

JOHN DONNE

1912

162. Grierson, Herbert J. C., editor. The Poems of John Donne. Edited from the old editions and numerous manuscripts, with introductions and commentary. In two volumes. Oxford: Clarendon.

163. Spearing, E. M. (Mrs. E. M. Simpson). "Donne's Sermons and Their Relation to His Poetry." *Modern Lanaguage Review*, 7: 40–53.

1913

164. Brooke, Rupert. "John Donne the Elizabethan." *Nation* (London), 12: 825–826.

165. De La Mare, Walter. "Elizabethan Poetry and Modern Poetry." *Edinburgh Review*, 217: 372–386.

166. Moore-Smith, G. C. "Donniana." *Modern Language Review*, 8: 47–52.

167. Spearing, E. M. (Mrs. E. M. Simpson). "A Chronological Arrangement of Donne's Sermons." *Modern Language Review*, 8: 468–483.

1914

168. Keynes, Geoffrey. The Bibliography of John Donne. 179 pp. London: Quaritch. [*See* No. 289.]

1916

169. Aronstein, Philip. "John Donne und Francis Bacon." *Englishe Studien*, 49: 360–376.

1917

170. Ramsay, Mary P. Les Doctrines médiévales chez Donne, le poète métaphysicien de l'Angleterre. 349 pp. London: Milford. [*See* No. 197.]

1919

171. Donne, John. Sermons: Selected Passages. With an essay by Logan Pearsall Smith. 314 pp. Oxford: Clarendon.

172. E. W. W. "Donne's Puns." *Times Literary Supplement*, December 11, page 750.

1920

173. Aronstein, Philip. "John Donne: a Study." *Anglia*, 44: 115–213. (Reprinted as John Donne als Dichter, Halle: Niemeyer, 1920).

174. Bailey, John. "The Sermons of a Poet." *Quarterly Review*, 233: 317–328.

175. "Donne's Sermons." *Nation* (London), 27: 247–248.

176. Lynd, Robert. "John Donne." *London Mercury*, 1: 435–447.

177. Moore-Smith, G. C. "Izaak Walton and John Donne." *Modern Language Review*, 15: 303.

1921

178. Donne, John. Sermons XV and LXVI. (Cambridge Plain Texts). 56 pp. Cambridge: University Press; New York: Macmillan.

179. Dunn, S. G. "The Authorship of 'Polydoron' (Ascribed to John Donne the Younger)." *Times Literary Supplement*, July 7, page 436.

180. Sampson, John. "A Contemporary Light upon John Donne (Annotation by Giles Oldisworth in a copy of the 1639 edition of Donne's poems)." *Essays and Studies of the English Association*, 7: 82–107.

1922

181. Donne, John. Selections. London: Cape.

182. Nethercot, A. H. "The Reputation of John Donne as a Metrist." *Sewanee Review*, 30: 463–474.

1923

183. Bredvold, Louis I. "The Naturalism of Donne in Relation to Some Renaissance Traditions." *Journal of English and Germanic Philology*, 22: 471–502.

184. Donne, John. Love Poems. With some account of his life taken from the writings of Izaak Walton. 114 pp. London: Nonesuch.

185. Donne, John. Paradoxes and Problemes: with Two Characters and an Essay of Valour. 88 pp. London: Nonesuch.

186. Eliot, T. S. "John Donne." *Nation* (London), 33: 331–332.

187. Forrest, H. T. S. The Five Authors of 'Shake-speares Sonnets.' 270 pp. London: Chapman & Dodd.

188. Jenkins, R. "Drayton's Relation to the School of Donne, as Revealed in the 'Shepheards Sirena.'" *Modern Language Association Publications*, 38: 557–587.

189. Keynes, Geoffrey. Bibliographical note to Devotions upon Emergent Occasions, edited by John Sparrow. Cambridge: University Press. [*See* No. 192.]

190. Keynes, Geoffrey, editor. Ten Sermons. Chosen from The Whole Body of Donne's Sermons. 162 pp. London: Nonesuch.

191. Simpson, Evelyn M. "John Donne and Sir Thomas Overbury's Characters." *Modern Language Review*, 18: 410–415.

192. Sparrow, John, editor. Devotions upon Emergent Occasions. With a bibliographical note by Geoffrey Keynes. 190 pp. Cambridge: University Press.

1924

193. Bredvold, Louis I. "Sir Thomas Egerton and Donne." *Times Literary Supplement*, March 13, page 160.

194. Fausset, Hugh I. John Donne: A Study in Discord. 318 pp. London: Cape.

195. George, Robert E. G. Outflying Philosophy . . . By Robert Sencourt (pseudonym). 358 pp. Hildesheim: F. Borgmeyer. (London: Simpkin Marshall, 1925.) [*See* No. 22.]

196. Hebel, J. W. "Drayton's 'Sirena.' " *Modern Language Association Publications*, 39: 814–836.

197. Ramsay, Mary P. Les Doctrines médiévales chez Donne, le poète métaphysicien de l'Angleterre. Second edition. 349 pp. London: Milford. [*See* No. 170.]

198. Simpson, Evelyn M. A Study of the Prose Works of John Donne. 374 pp. Oxford: Clarendon.

199. Sparrow, John. "On the Date of Donne's 'Hymne to God my God, in my sickness.' " *Modern Language Review*, 19: 462–466.

1925

200. Bredvold, Louis I. "The Religious Thought of Donne in Relation to Medieval and Later Traditions," and "Studies in Shakespeare, Milton, and Donne." *University of Michigan Publications, Language and Literature*, 1: 191–232. Ann Arbor, Michigan.

201. Binyon, Laurence. "A Study of Donne." *Bookman* (London), 67: 201–202.

202. De Havilland, M. "Two Unpublished Manuscripts of John Donne." *London Mercury*, 13: 159–162.

203. "Donne's Poems: Concerning the Authorship of 'Absence, hear thou my protestation.' " *New Statesman*, 26: 80.

204. Grierson, Herbert J. C. "Donne's Poems: the Authorship of 'Absence.' " *New Statesman*, 26: 108.

205. "John Donne." *Contemporary Review*, 127: 669–671.

206. Praz, Mario. Secentismo e Marinismo in Inghilterra: John Donne—Richard Crashaw. 306 pp. Florence: La Voce.

1926

207. Chambers, E. K., editor. The Poems of John Donne.
With an introduction by George Saintsbury. In two
volumes (Reprint of 1896 ed.) London: Routledge.

208. Donne, John. Devotions upon Emergent Occasions,
together with Death's Duel. Introduction by William
H. Draper. (Abbey Classics.) 258 pp. London:
Simpkin.

209. Donne, John. The First Anniuersarie: An Anatomie
of the World; [and] The Second Anniuersarie: Of
the Progres of the Soule. (This was issued in 1927 by
Payson & Clarke and was later issued as No. 26 of the
Publications of the Facsimile Text Society.) [See Nos.
219 and 303.]

210. Draper, William H. Introduction to Devotions upon
Emergent Occasions, together with Death's Duel.
(Abbey Classics.) 258 pp. London: Simpkin. [See
No. 208.]

211. Hamilton, George R. "Wit and Beauty: a Study of
Metaphysical Poetry (Donne and Francis Thompson)." London Mercury, 14: 606–620.

212. Lucas, F. L. "John Donne." Authors Dead and Living,
pages 54–61. London: Chatto and Windus.

213. Mégroz, R. L. "The Wit and Fantasy of Donne."
Dublin Magazine, April, pages 47–51.

214. Mitchell, F. L. "Jack Donne, the Pagan; Doctor
John Donne, the Divine." Bookman's Journal, 14:
15–18.

215. Payne, F. W. John Donne and His Poetry. 167 pp.
(Poetry and Life Series.) London: Harrap.

216. Saintsbury, George. Introduction, The Poems of John
Donne, edited by E. K. Chambers. In two volumes.
(Reprint of 1896 ed.) London: Routledge. [See No .207.]

217. Simpson, Evelyn M. " 'Essays in Divinity' (Cancelled dedication to Sir Harry Vane, Jr.)." *Times Literary Supplement*, January 21, page 44.

218. Wilder, M. L. "Did Jonson Write 'The Expostulation' Attributed to Donne?" *Modern Language Review*, 21: 431–435.

1927

219. Donne, John. The First Anniuersarie: An Anatomie of the World; [and] The Second Anniuersarie: Of the Progres of the Soule. (Replica.) 54+49 pp. New York: Payson & Clarke. [The same as Nos. 209 and 303.]

220. Donne, John. Poems. (Augustan Books of English Poetry.) 31 pp. London: Benn.

221. Potter, G. R. "Milton's Early Poems: the School of Donne and the Elizabethan Sonneteers." *Philological Quarterly*, 6: 396–400.

222. Robbie, H. J. L. "Undescribed Manuscript of Donne's Poems." *Review of English Studies*, 3: 415–419.

223. Simpson, Evelyn M. "Two Manuscripts of Donne's 'Paradoxes and Problemes'." *Review of English Studies*, 3: 129–145.

224. Williamson, George. "The Talent of T. S. Eliot: a Study of Donne's Influence." *Sewanee Review*, 35: 284–295. (Reprinted and expanded in University of Washington Chapbooks, 1929.) [*See* No. 246.]

225. Wilson, F. P. "Notes on the Early Life of John Donne." *Review of English Studies*, 3: 272–279.

1928

226. Cole, G. D. H., and M. I. Cole, editors. Selected Shorter Poems. (Ormond Poets.) 65 pp. London: Douglas.

227. Dark, Sidney. "John Donne." Five Deans: John Colet, John Donne, Jonathan Swift, Arthur Penrhyn Stanley, William Ralph Inge. London: Cape.

228. Johnson, B. "Classical Allusions in the Poetry of Donne." *Modern Language Association Publications*, 43: 1098–1109.

229. Legouis, Pierre. Donne the Craftsman: the Structure of the Songs and Sonnets. 98 pp. (Paris: Didier.) Oxford: University Press.

230. MacCarthy, Desmond. "A Reader's Bibliography of John Donne." *Life and Letters*, 1: 156–160; 433.

231. Robbie, H. J. L. "Two More Undescribed Manuscripts of John Donne's Poems: B. M. Harleian 3998 and Dobell MS." *Review of English Studies*, 4: 214–216.

232. Simpson, Evelyn M. "A Note On Donne's Punctuation." *Review of English Studies*, 4: 295–300.

233. Sparrow, John. "Donne's Table-Talk." *London Mercury*, 18: 39–46.

234. Terrill, T. E. "A Note on John Donne's Early Reading." *Modern Language Notes*, 43: 318–319.

235. Terrill, T. E. Spanish Influence on John Donne. Unpublished Harvard dissertation.

236. Williamson, George. "The Nature of the Donne Tradition." *Studies in Philology*, 25: 416–438.

237. Wrightson, Rodger. "A Note on Donne's Poetry." *Bookman's Journal*, 16: 373–379.

1929

238. Cogan, Isabel. "John Donne: Poet and Metaphysician." *Poetry Review*, 20: 183–194.

239. Donne, John. An Anatomie of the World. 32 pp. Shaftesbury, Dorset: High House Press.

240. Frost, A. C. "John Donne and a Modern Poet (T. S. Eliot)." *Cambridge Review*, 50: 449–450.

241. Grierson, Herbert J. C. "Donne and Lucretius." *Times Literary Supplement*, December 5, page 1032.

242. Grierson, Herbert J. C., editor. The Poems of John Donne. Edited from the old editions and numerous manuscripts, with introductions and commentary. 460 pp. Oxford: Clarendon.

243. Hayward, John, editor. The Complete Poetry and Selected Prose of John Donne. 793 pp. London: Nonesuch; New York: Random House.

244. Spencer, Theodore, editor. John Donne's Letter to Sir Nicholas Carey, written from his house in London in the early summer of the plague year 1625, and printed from the original manuscript, which is preserved in the Charles Eliot Norton Collection of Donne's writings, which is now a part of the Harvard College Library. Cambridge, Massachusetts.

245. Terrill, T. E. "Spanish Influence on John Donne." *Harvard University Summaries of Theses*, pages 177–178. [*See* No. 235.]

246. Williamson, George. The Talent of T. S. Eliot: a Study of Donne and Eliot. 37 pp. University of Washington Chapbooks, No. 32. (Reprinted from *Sewanee Review*, 1927.) [*See* No. 224.]

1930

247. Butt, J. E. "John Donne and Lincoln's Inn." *Times Literary Supplement*, April 10, page 318.

248. Donne, John. Biathanatos, reproduced from the first edition, with a biographical note by J. W. Hebel. 218 pp. New York: Facsimile Text Society; Oxford: Blackwell.

249. Donne, John. Defense of Women for Their Inconstancy and Their Paintings. 12 pp. Limited edition. London: Simpkin.

250. Grierson, Herbert J. C., and C. Sisson. "Second Satyre: Emendation." *Times Literary Supplement*, February 20, page 142; March 6, page 190; March 13, page 214.

251. Hebel, J. W. Biographical note to Biathanatos, pages v–vii. New York: Facsimile Text Society; Oxford: Blackwell. [*See* No. 248.]

252. Shapiro, I. A. "John Donne and Lincoln's Inn." *Times Literary Supplement*, October 16, page 833; October 23, page 861.

253. Simpson, Evelyn M., editor. Courtiers Library, or Catalogus librorum aulicorum incomparabilium et non vendibilium, by John Donne. With translation. Limited edition. 93 pp. London: Nonesuch.

254. Sisson, C., and Herbert J. C. Grierson. "Second Satyre: Emendation." *Times Literary Supplement*, February 20, page 142; March 6, page 190; March 13, page 214.

255. Sparrow, John. "Donne and Contemporary Preachers." *Essays and Studies of the English Association*, 16: 144–178.

256. Williamson, George. The Donne Tradition. A study in English Poetry from Donne to the death of Cowley. 264 pp. Cambridge, Massachusetts: Harvard University Press; Oxford: University Press.

257. Willmore, M. O. "John Donne." *London Quarterly Review*, 153: 109–111.

258. Wood, H. Harvey. "A Seventeenth Century Manuscript of Poems by Donne and Others." *Essays and Studies of the English Association*, 16: 179–190.

1931

259. Addleshaw, S. "A Famous Dean: Doctor John Donne of St. Paul's." *Church Quarterly Review*, 113: 38–54.

260. Bennett, R. E. "John Manningham and Donne's 'Paradoxes.'" *Modern Language Notes*, 46: 309–313.

261. Bensly, Edward, and A. C. Howell. "Query on Sermon XXX, Folio of 1640." *Notes and Queries*, 161: 156–157, 230.

262. Chambers, E. K. "An Elegy by John Donne." *Review of English Studies*, 7: 69–71.

263. Deas, M. C. "A Note on Rowland Woodward, the Friend of Donne." *Review of English Studies*, 7: 454–457.

264. Elliott, G. R. "John Donne: the Middle Phase." *Bookman* (New York), 73: 337–346.

265. Fausset, Hugh I., editor. The Poems of John Donne. (Everyman editions.) 320 pp. London: Dent; New York: Dutton.

266. Fausset, Hugh I. "A Poet and His Vision." *Bookman* (London), 79: 341–342.

267. Grierson, Herbert J. C. "Donne and the Roman Poets." *Times Literary Supplement*, February 26, page 154.

268. Howell, A. C., and Edward Bensly. "Query on Sermon XXX, Folio of 1640." *Notes and Queries*, 161: 156–157, 230.

269. Hutchinson, F. E. "Donne the Preacher." *Theology*, March, pages 155–163.

270. "In Memory of John Donne." *Bookman* (London), 79: 341–347. (Includes Nos. 266, 273, 278, and 283.)

271. "John Donne." *Times Literary Supplement*, March 26, pages 241–242.

272. "John Donne, Preacher and Bencher of Lincoln's Inn." *The Times*, March 31.

273. Leavis, F. R. "The Influence of John Donne on Modern Poetry." *Bookman* (London), 79: 346–347.

274. Lindsay, Jack. "The Date of Donne's 'Autumnall' Elegy." *Times Literary Supplement*, March 19, page 234.

275. Lindsay, Jack. "Donne and the Roman Poets." *Times Literary Supplement*, February 19, page 135.

276. Nicholls, N. "The Early Editions of John Donne." *Bookman* (London), 79: 370–371.

277. Porter, A. "Dean Donne." *Spectator*, 146: 539–540.

278. Saltmarshe, C. "The Man and his Vision." *Bookman* (London), 79: 343–344.

279. Shapiro, I. A. "The Text of Donne's 'Letters to Severall Persons.'" *Review of English Studies*, 7: 291–301.

280. Sparrow, John. "A Book from Donne's Library: 'Epigrammata et poematia vetera, edited by P. Pithous and printed at Paris in 1590.'" *London Mercury*, 25: 171–180.

281. Sparrow, John. "Donne's Religious Development." *Theology*, March, pages 144–154.

282. Spencer, Theodore, editor. A Garland for John Donne, 1631–1931. Essays by T. S. Eliot, Evelyn M. Simpson, Mario Praz, John Hayward, Mary P. Ramsay, John Sparrow, George Williamson, and Theodore Spencer. 202 pp. Cambridge, Massachusetts: Harvard University Press; Oxford: University Press.

283. Tompkinson, Cyril. "A Note on the Personal Religion of John Donne." *Bookman* (London), 79: 345–346.

284. Wood, H. Harvey. "Donne's 'Mr. Tilman': a Postscript." *Times Literary Supplement*, July 9, page 547.

1932

285. Bald, R. C. Donne's Influence in English Literature. 62 pp. Morpeth: St. John's College Press.

286. Butt, J. E. "Walton's Copy of Donne's Letters." *Review of English Studies*, 8: 72–74.

287. Greene, G. S. "Drummond's Borrowings from Donne." *Philological Quarterly*, 11: 26–38.

288. Hughes, M. Y. "The Lineage of the 'Extasie.' " *Modern Language Review*, 27: 1–5.

289. Keynes, Geoffrey. The Bibliography of Doctor John Donne. Second edition. 311 pp. Cambridge: University Press. [*See* No. 168.]

290. Legouis, Pierre. "Sur un vers de Donne." *Revue Anglo-Américaine*, 10: 49–50, 228–230.

291. Shapiro, I. A. "John Donne and Parliament." *Times Literary Supplement*, March 10, page 172.

292. Williamson, George. "The Donne Canon." *Times Literary Supplement*, August 18, page 581.

293. Woolf, Virginia. "Donne after Three Centuries." The Second Common Reader, pages 20–37. London: Leonard and Virginia Woolf.

1933

294. Bennett, R. E. "Addition to Donne's 'Catalogus librorum.' " *Modern Language Notes*, 48: 167–168.

295. Grierson, Herbert J. C., editor. The Poems of John Donne. 460 pp. Oxford: Clarendon. (Reprint of 1929 edition.) [*See* No. 242.]

296. Haddow, G. C. "Donne's Prose." *Queen's Quarterly*, 40: 87–98.

297. Kortemme, J. Das Verhältnis John Donne zur Scholastik und zum Barock. Eine Untersuchung zu den Anfängen des englischen Barocks. 85 pp. Münster: Druck der Westfälischen Versinsdruckerei Akt.-Ges.

298. Simpson, Evelyn M., editor. Donne's Sermon of Valediction at his going into Germany, preached at Lincoln's Inn, April 18, 1619, printed from the original version in the Lothian and Ashmole manuscripts, and from XXVI Sermons. Limited edition. 81 pp. London: Nonesuch; New York: Random House.

1934

299. Bennett, Joan. Four Metaphysical Poets: Donne, Herbert, Vaughan, and Crashaw. 135 pp. Cambridge: University Press.

300. Brooks, Harold. "Donne and Drant." *Times Literary Supplement*, August 16, page 565.

301. Coffin, Charles M. "Bibliography of Donne." *Times Literary Supplement*, August 2, page 541.

302. Doggett, Frank A. "Donne's Platonism." *Sewanee Review*, 42: 274–292.

303. Donne, John. The First Anniuersarie: An Anatomie of the World; [and] The Second Anniuersarie: Of the Progres of the Soule. (Replica; No. 26 of the Publications of the Facsimile Text Society.) 54+49 pp. New York: Columbia University Press. [This is the same as Nos. 209 and 219.]

304. Donne, John. Love Poems. New Rochelle, New York: Peter Pauper Press.

305. Grønbech, Vilhelm. Mystikere: Europa og Indien. Del Donne, Wordsworth, Herder. (Udg. med Understöttelse of Carlsbergfondet). 260 pp. Copenhagen: Brauner.

306. Hughes, M. Y. "Kidnapping Donne." *University of California Publications in English*, 4: 61–89.

307. Leishman, James B. The Metaphysical Poets: Donne, Herbert, Vaughan, Traherne. 239 pp. Oxford: Clarendon.

308. Lewis, E. Glyn. "Donne's Third Satyre." *Times Literary Supplement*. September 6, page 604; September 27, page 655.

309. Lewis, E. Glyn. "Interpretation of Donne's Elegie 'The dreame.' " *Modern Language Review*, 29: 436–440.

310. Lindsay, Jack. "Donne and Drant." *Times Literary Supplement*, August 23, page 577.

311. Lindsay, Jack. "Donne's Third Satyre." *Times Literary Supplement*, September 20, page 636.

312. Potter, G. R. "Donne's Discovery of Himself." *University of California Publications in English*, 4: 3–23.

313. Reeves, George B. "The Microcosm in the Works of John Donne." *Abstracts of Theses, University of Pittsburgh*, 10: 554–555.

314. Scholderer, V. "Donne and Drant." *Times Literary Supplement*, August 30, page 589.

315. Simpson, Evelyn M. "More Manuscripts of Donne's 'Paradoxes and Problems.' " *Review of English Studies*, 10: 288–300; 10: 412–416.

316. Taggard, G. "John Donne: a Link between the Seventeenth and the Twentieth Centuries." *Scholastic*, 24: 11–12.

317. Umbach, Herbert H. The Easter Sermons of John Donne. An edition with introduction, commentary, textual notes, and a bibliography. Ithaca, New York: Cornell University.

318. Williamson, George. "The Libertine Donne: Comments on 'Biathanatos.' " *Philological Quarterly*, 13: 276–291.

1935

319. Alexander, H. "John Donne, Poet and Divine." *Queen's Quarterly*, 42: 471–481.

320. Bennett, R. E. "Donne and Sir Thomas Roe." *Times Literary Supplement*, January 31, page 62.

321. Matsuura, Kaichi. "Lyrical Poems of John Donne." *Studies in English Literature* (Imperial University, Tokyo), 15: 58–67.

322. Maxwell, H., and R. S. B. "John Donne's 'All Tincture.' " *Notes and Queries*, 168: 62, 104.

323. Maxwell, Ian R. "John Donne's Library." *Times Literary Supplement*, July 11, page 448.

324. Nicolson, Marjorie. "The New Astronomy and English Literary Imagination." *Studies in Philology*, 32: 428–462.

325. Nicolson, Marjorie. "The Telescope and Imagination." *Modern Philology*, 32: 233–260.

326. Shapiro, I. A. "Donne and Sir Thomas Roe." *Times Literary Supplement*, February 7, page 76.

327. Simpson, Percy. "A Book from the Library of John Donne." *Oriel Record*, January.

328. Smalley, Donald A. "Browning and Donne." *Times Literary Supplement*, October 10, page 631.

329. Wasilifsky, Adolph M. "John Donne the Rhetor, a Study of the Tropes and Figures of the St. Paul Sermons." *Cornell University Abstracts of Theses*.

1936

330. Baldenne, F. (pseudonym of F. Baldensperger), translator. "Aubade; Chanson; Constance feminine; Infini d'amour; Ta fièvre; Message; Sorcellerie par image; Le gage." *Revue de Littérature Comparée*, 16: 710–716.

331. Bennett, R. E. Bibliographical note to Juvenilia, or Certain Paradoxes and Problems [4 pages]. New York: Facsimile Text Society. [*See* No. 332.]

332. Donne, John. Juvenilia, or Certain Paradoxes and Problems, reproduced from the first edition, with a bibliographical note by R. E. Bennett. 104 pp. New York: Facsimile Text Society.

333. Moore, J. F. "Scholasticism, Donne, and the Metaphysical Conceit." *Revue Anglo-Américaine*, 13: 289–297.

334. Newdigate, B. H. "An Overlooked Poem by John Donne? 'To his friend Captaine John Smith.'" *London Mercury*, 33: 424–425.

335. Potter, G. R. "Donne's 'Extasie': contra Legouis." *Philological Quarterly*, 15: 247–253.

336. Sampson, A. "The Resurrection of Donne." *London Mercury*, 33: 307–314.

337. Teager, F. S. "The Patronage of Joseph Hall and John Donne by Sir Robert Drury." *Philological Quarterly*, 15: 408–413.

338. White, Helen C. The Metaphysical Poets: a Study in Religious Experience. 444 pp. New York: Macmillan.

1937

339. Ashley-Montagu, M. F. "Donne the Astronomer." *Times Literary Supplement*, page 576.

340. Bald, R. C. "Three Metaphysical Epigrams." *Philological Quarterly*, 16: 405.

341. Bennett, R. E. "Tracts from John Donne's Library." *Review of English Studies*, 13: 333–335.

342. Bennett, R. E. "Walton's Use of Donne's Letters." *Philological Quarterly*, 16: 30–34.

343. Coffin, Charles M. "Donne's Astronomy." *Times Literary Supplement*, September 18, page 675.

344. Coffin, Charles M. John Donne and the New Philosophy. 311 pp. New York: Columbia University Press.

345. Donne, John. Love Poems of John Donne. (Zodiac books.) 61 pp. London: Chatto and Windus.

346. Douds, John B. "Donne's Technique of Dissonance." *Modern Language Association Publications*, 52: 1051–1061.

347. Grierson, Herbert J. C., editor. The Poems of John Donne. (Oxford Standard Authors.) 460 pp. Oxford: Clarendon. (Reprint of 1929 edition.) [*See* No. 242.]

348. Legouis, Pierre. "John Donne." *Times Literary Supplement*, July 31, page 560.

349. Lindsay, Jack. "Donne and Blake." *Times Literary Supplement*, July 24, page 544.

350. Mitchell, W. F. "John Donne the Astronomer." *Times Literary Supplement*, July 10, page 512; August 7, page 576.

351. Rugoff, Milton A. "Drummond's Debt to Donne." *Philological Quarterly*, 16: 85–88.

352. Shapiro, I. A. "Donne a Tychonian?" *Times Literary Supplement*, July 17, page 528.

353. Shapiro, I. A. "John Donne." *Times Literary Supplement*, August 14, page 592.

354. Shapiro, I. A. "John Donne the Astronomer and the Date of the Eighth Problem." *Times Literary Supplement*, July 3, page 492.

355. Umbach, Herbert H. "The Rhetoric of Donne's Sermons." *Modern Language Association Publications*, 52: 354–358.

1938

356. Bennett, Joan. "The Love Poetry of John Donne. A Reply to Mr. Lewis." Seventeenth Century Studies Presented to Sir Herbert Grierson, pages 85–104. Oxford: Clarendon.

357. Lewis, C. S. "Donne and Love Poetry in the Seventeenth Century." Seventeenth Century Studies Presented to Sir Herbert Grierson, pages 64–84. Oxford: Clarendon.

358. Lewis, E. Glyn. "The Question of Toleration in the Works of John Donne." *Modern Language Review*, 33: 255–258.

359. Shapiro, I. A. "Donne and Astronomy." *Modern Language Review*, 33: 280–281.

360. Ransom, John Crowe. "Shakespeare at Sonnets." *Southern Review*, 3: 531–553. (Reprinted in The World's Body. New York: Scribner's, 1938.)

EDWARD, LORD HERBERT OF CHERBURY

1923

361. Moore-Smith, G. C., editor. The Poems, English and Latin, of Edward, Lord Herbert of Cherbury. (Oxford English Texts.) 204 pp. Oxford: Clarendon.

1925

362. Hebel, J. W. "A Divine Love [poem] Addressed by Lord Herbert to Lady Bedford?" *Modern Language Review*, 20: 74–76.

1926

363. Grierson, Herbert J. C. "Edward, Lord Herbert." *Modern Language Review*, 21: 210–213.

1928

364. The Autobiography of Edward, Lord Herbert of Cherbury. With an introduction by C. H. Herford. 109 pp. Newtown, Montgomeryshire: Gregynog Press.

1931

365. Howarth, R. G., editor. Minor Poets of the Seventeenth Century: Suckling, Lovelace, Carew & Herbert [of Cherbury]. 414 pp. London: Dent.

1933

366. Chapman, R. W. "Lord Herbert of Cherbury and the Bodleian." *Bodleian Quarterly Record*, 7: 174–175.

367. Wright, Herbert G. "An Unpublished Manuscript by Lord Herbert of Cherbury, Entitled 'Religio Laici.' " *Modern Language Review*, 28: 295–307.

1934

368. Pilley, John G. "Mersenne and Herbert." *Times Literary Supplement*, February 15, page 108.

1935

369. Lyttle, Charles. "Lord Herbert of Cherbury, Apostle of Ethical Theism." *Church History*, 4: 247–267.

1937

370. Carré, Meyrick H., translator. De Veritate. Translated from the 1645 edition. (University of Bristol Studies, No. 6.) 334 pp. Bristol: Arrowsmith.

GEORGE HERBERT

1912

371. Tallentyre, S. G. "Parson-Poets." *North American Review*, 195: 84–90.

1915

372. Beeching, H. C., editor. The Country Parson. 228 pp. New York: Longmans; Oxford: Blackwell. (Reprint of 1898 edition.)

373. Currier, Albert H. "George Herbert." Biographical and Literary Studies, pages 183–208. Boston: The Pilgrim Press.

1916

374. Herbert, George. The Priest to the Temple; or, The Country Parson, His Character and Rule of Life. With an introduction by the Bishop of North Carolina. Milwaukee, Wisconsin: Morehouse.

375. Palmer, George H., editor. The English Poems of George Herbert. 439 pp. New York: Houghton Mifflin.

1918

376. "George Herbert." *Living Age*, 296: 813–815.

1920

377. Palmer, George H., editor. The English Works of George Herbert. Newly arranged and annotated and considered in relation to his life. Three volumes. London: Hodder. (Reprint of 1905 edition.)

1921

378. Clutton-Brock, Arthur. "George Herbert." More Essays on Books. London: Methuen; New York: Dutton.

379. Merrill, L. R. "The 'Church Porch': closing sentiment possibly derived from Nicholas Grimald's 'Musorius, the Philosopher's Saying' in Tottell's Miscellany." *Modern Language Notes*, 36: 249–250.

1923

380. Herbert, George. Poems. Selected by Sir H. Walford Davies. Newtown: Montgomeryshire: Gregynog Press.

1925

381. Stenberg, Theodore P. "Wordsworth's 'Happy Warrior' and Herbert's 'Constancy.'" *Modern Language Notes*, 40: 252–253.

1927

382. Herbert, George. Poems. (Augustan Books of English Poetry.) 31 pp. London: Benn.

383. Herbert, George. The Temple and A Priest to the Temple. Introduction by Edward Thomas. (Everyman's Library.) 305 pp. London: Dent.

384. Herbert, George. Works in Prose and Verse. (Chandos Classics.) 504 pp. London: Warne.

385. Mann, Cameron. A Concordance to the English Poems of George Herbert. 289 pp. New York: Houghton Mifflin.

386. Meynell, Francis, editor. The Temple. 224 pp. London: Nonesuch; New York: Random House.

1928

387. Lucas, F. L. "George Herbert." *Life and Letters*, 1: 548–561.

388. Naylor, E. W. "Three Seventeenth Century Poet-Parsons (Thomas Traherne, George Herbert, Robert Herrick) and Music." *Proceedings of the Musical Association* (London), 54: 93–113.

389. Robbie, H. J. L. "George Herbert." *Church Quarterly Review*, 105: 359–364.

1932

390. Beachcroft, T. O. "Nicholas Ferrar: his Influence on and Friendship with George Herbert." *Criterion*, 12: 24–42.

391. Eliot, T. S. "George Herbert." *Spectator*, 148: 360–361.

392. Hall, Bernard G. "The 'Jacula Prudentum.'" *Times Literary Supplement*, April 21, page 291.

1933

393. Blunden, Edmund. "George Herbert's Latin Poems." *Essays and Studies of the English Association*, 19: 29–39.

394. "George Herbert." *Times Literary Supplement*, March 2, pages 133–134.

395. "George Herbert, 1593–1633." *Cambridge Review*, 54: 291–293.

396. Hall, Bernard G. "The Text of George Herbert." *Times Literary Supplement*, October 26, page 731.

397. Hutchinson, F. E. "George Herbert: A Tercentenary." *Nineteenth Century*, 113: 358–368.

398. Orange, U. M. D. "Herbert's Poetry." *Poetry Review*, 24: 118–127.

399. Slade, Hilda M. "The Tercentenary of George Herbert." *Poetry Review*, 24: 115–117.

400. Sparrow, John. "The Text of George Herbert." *Times Literary Supplement*, December 14, page 896.

401. Thomas, Gilbert. "George Herbert." *Contemporary Review*, 143: 706–716.

1934

402. Barrett, K. I. Studies in the Life and Writings of George Herbert. Unpublished dissertation, University of London.

403. Bennett, Joan. Four Metaphysical Poets: Donne, Herbert, Vaughan, and Crashaw. 135 pp. Cambridge: University Press.

404. Brulé, A. "Un poème latin de George Herbert." *Revue Anglo-Américaine*, 12: 49–51.

405. Leishman, James B. The Metaphysical Poets: Donne, Herbert, Vaughan, Traherne. 239 pp. Oxford: Clarendon.

1935

406. Wright, Herbert G. "Was George Herbert the Author of 'Jacula Prudentum'?" *Review of English Studies*, 11: 139–144.

1936

407. Harper, G. M. "George Herbert's Poems." *Quarterly Review*, 267: 58–73.
408. Hutchinson, F. E. "John Wesley and George Herbert." *London Quarterly Review*, 161: 439–455.
409. Warren, Austin. "George Herbert." *American Review*, 7: 249–271.
410. White, Helen C. The Metaphysical Poets: a Study in Religious Experience. 444 pp. New York: Macmillan.

1937

411. Butts, M. "The Heresy Game." *Spectator*, 158: 466–467.
412. Luke, S. "An Old Handbook on the Pastoral Office: Discussion of George Herbert's 'A Priest to the Temple.' " *London Quarterly Review*, 162: 198–206.

1938

413. Hayes, A. McH. "Counterpoint in Herbert." *Studies in Philology*, 35: 43–60.
414. Hutchinson, Rev. F. E. "George Herbert." Seventeenth Century Studies Presented to Sir Herbert Grierson, pages 148–160. Oxford: Clarendon.

HENRY KING

1913

415. Mason, Lawrence. "The Life and Works of Henry King, D.D." *Transactions of the Connecticut Academy of Arts and Sciences*, 18: 225–289.

1914

416. Mason, Lawrence, editor. The English Poems of Henry King, D.D., 1592–1669, sometime Bishop of Chichester. 241 pp. New Haven: Yale University Press.

1917

417. Mason, Lawrence. "Bishop Henry King and the Oxford Dictionary." *Modern Language Notes*, 32: 55–57.

1921

418. Saintsbury, George, editor. Minor Poets of the Caroline Period. In three volumes. Volume Three: Cleveland, King, Stanley, Flatman, Whiting. Oxford: University Press.

1925

419. Sparrow, John, editor. The Poems of Bishop Henry King. 227 pp. London: Nonesuch.

1929

420. Simpson, Percy. "The Bodleian Manuscripts of Henry King." *Bodleian Quarterly Record*, 5: 324–340.

ANDREW MARVELL

1913

421. Bickley, F. "The Quality of Marvell's Poetry." *North American Review*, 197: 235–245.

1918

422. Meynell, Francis, editor. The Best of Both Worlds. A choice taken from the poems of Andrew Marvell and Henry Vaughan. 60 pp. London: Allen and Unwin.

1920

423. "Marvell and Lucan: Parallels between his 'Ode to Cromwell' and the Pharsalia." *Times Literary Supplement*, January 29, page 69; February 5, page 86.

1921

424. Affable Hawk (pseudonym of Desmond MacCarthy.) "Andrew Marvell—Centenary." *New Statesman*, 16: 757.
425. "Andrew Marvell." *Nation* (London), 29: 20–21.
426. Clutton-Brock, Arthur. "Andrew Marvell." More Essays on Books. London: Methuen; New York: Dutton.
427. Falls, Cyril. "Andrew Marvell." *Nineteenth Century*, 89: 630–642. (Reprinted in The Critic's Armoury, 1924.)

1922

428. Bagguley, William, editor. Andrew Marvell, 1621–1678. Tercentenary tributes by Augustine Birrell, H. Hensley Henson, T. S. Eliot, Cyril Falls, Edmund Gosse, Harold J. Massingham, J. C. Squire, and Edward Wright. 131 pp. London: Milford.
429. Hodgson, G. E. "Andrew Marvell, an Appreciation." *Poetry Review*, 13: 179–183.
430. Margoliouth, H. M. "Andrew Marvell: Some Biographical Points." *Modern Language Review*, 17: 351–361.
431. Sheppard, Thomas. Andrew Marvell Tercentenary Celebrations at Hull. 21 pp. Hull: Brown.

1923

432. Legouis, Pierre. "Andrew Marvell: Further Biographical Points." *Modern Language Review*, 18: 416–426.
433. Legouis, Pierre. "Marvell et Swift." *Revue Anglo-Américaine*, 1: 240–242.

434. Marvell, Andrew. Miscellaneous Poems. 148 pp. London: Nonesuch.

1924

435. Falls, Cyril. "Andrew Marvell." The Critic's Armoury, pages 39–60. London: Cobden-Sanderson. [*See* No. 427.]
436. Margoliouth, H. M. "Marvell in Rome." *Times Literary Supplement*, June 5, page 356.

1925

437. Marvell, Andrew. Poems. (Augustan Books of English Poetry.) 31 pp. London: Benn.

1926

438. Legouis, Pierre. "Marvell's 'Maniban.'" *Review of English Studies*, 2: 328–335.
439. Lucas, F. L. "Andrew Marvell." Authors Dead and Living, pages 76–81. London: Chatto and Windus.
440. Margoliouth, H. M. "Andrew Marvell, Senior." *Review of English Studies*, 2: 96–97.

1927

441. Margoliouth, H. M., editor. The Poems and Letters of Andrew Marvell. (Oxford English Texts.) In two volumes. Oxford: University Press.

1928

442. Cole, G. D. H., and M. I. Cole, editors. Poems. (Ormond Poets.) 64 pp. London: Douglas.
443. Legouis, Pierre. André Marvell, poète, puritain, patriote, 1621–1678. 523 pp. (Paris: Didier) Oxford: University Press.

1929

444. Sackville-West, V. Andrew Marvell. 64 pp. London: Faber.

1930

445. Woledge, G. "Saint Amand, Fairfax, and Marvell."
     Modern Language Review, 25: 481–483.

1932

446. Empson, William. "Marvell's 'Garden.' " *Scrutiny*,
     7: 236–240. (Reprinted in Determinations. London,
     1934.) [*See* No. 448].

1933

447. Lawrence, C. E. "The Caged Eagle: a Drama."
     Bookman (London), 84: 277–279.

1934

448. Empson, William. "Marvell's 'Garden'." Determi-
     nations, edited by F. R. Leavis. London: Chatto and
     Windus. (Reprint of article in *Scrutiny*, 1932.) [*See*
     No. 446.]

449. Legouis, Pierre, "Marvell and Addison: a Note to
     No. 89 of 'The Spectator.' " *Review of English Studies*,
     10: 447–450.

1935

450. Richards, I. T. "Note on Source Influences in Shel-
     ley's 'Cloud' and 'Skylark.' " *Modern Language Associ-
     ation Publications*, 50: 562–567.

1936

451. Robbins, Caroline. "Note on a Hitherto Unprinted
     Speech by Andrew Marvell." *Modern Language Review*,
     31: 549–550.

1937

452. Marvell, Andrew. Miscellaneous Poems. 47 pp. Lon-
     don: Chatto and Windus.

KATHERINE PHILIPS

1921

453. Bensly, Edward. "Lucasia." *Notes and Queries*, Ser. 12, Vol. 8; page 68.

1926

454. McKeehan, I. P. "Neglected Example of the 'In Memoriam' Stanza." *Modern Language Notes*, 41: 531–532.

1928

455. Gosse, Edmund. "The Matchless Orinda." Selected Essays, Volume One, pages 103–136. London: Heinemann.

1931

456. Souers, Philip W. The Matchless Orinda. 334 pp. Cambridge, Massachusetts: Harvard University Press; London: Milford.

1937

457. Alspach, R. K. "The Matchless Orinda." *Modern Language Notes*, 52: 116–117.

THOMAS TRAHERNE

1913

458. Lock, W. "An English Mystic." *Constructive Quarterly*, 1: 826–836.

1914

459. Jones, Rufus M. "Thomas Traherne and The Spiritual Poets of the Seventeenth Century." Spiritual Reformers in The 16th & 17th Centuries, pages 320–335. London: Macmillan.

1917

460. Proud, J. W. "Thomas Traherne: a Divine Philosopher." *Friends' Quarterly Examiner*, 51: 65–82.

1919

461. Sherer, G. R. "More and Traherne." *Modern Language Notes*, 34: 49–50.
462. Willett, Gladys E. Traherne: an Essay. 57 pp. Cambridge: Heffer.

1920

463. Towers, F. "Thomas Traherne: His Outlook on Life." *Nineteenth Century*, 87: 1024–1030.
464. Willett, Gladys E. "Traherne." *Spectator*, 124: 84–85.

1922

465. Parker, S. T. H. "The Riches of Thomas Traherne." *Living Age*, 314: 223–225.
466. Payne, Arthur. "A Prose Poet. Thomas Traherne." *Educational Times*, 4: 347.

1926

467. Dobell, Bertram, editor. Centuries of Meditation. 343 pp. London: Dobell. (Reprint of 1908 edition.)

1927

468. Dawson, M. L. "Thomas Traherne." *Times Literary Supplement*, September 29, page 667.
469. Hopkinson, A. W. "Thomas Traherne." *Times Literary Supplement*, October 6, page 694.
470. Price, C. "Thomas Traherne." *Times Literary Supplement*, October 27, page 767.
471. Watkins, Alfred. "Thomas Traherne." *Times Literary Supplement*, October 20, page 742.

1928

472. Naylor, E. W. "Three Seventeenth Century Poet-Parsons (Thomas Traherne, George Herbert, Robert Herrick) and Music." *Proceedings of Musical Association* (London), 54: 93–113.

1929

473. Thompson, Elbert N. S. "The Philosophy of Thomas Traherne." *Philological Quarterly*, 8: 97–112.

1930

474. Beachcroft, T. O. "Traherne and the Cambridge Platonists." *Dublin Review*, 186: 278–290.
475. Beachcroft, T. O. "Traherne and the Doctrine of Felicity." *Criterion*, 9: 291–307.
476. Löhrer, Frieda. Die Mystik und ihre Quellen in Thomas Traherne. 168 pp. Zürich: Buchdruckerei Rheintaler Volksfreund Au.

1931

477. Wade, Gladys I. "The Manuscripts of the Poems of Thomas Traherne." *Modern Language Review*, 26: 401–407.

1932

478. Christ, Ernst. Studien zu Thomas Traherne. 69 pp. Tübingen: E. Göbel.
479. Grigson, G. "The Transports of Thomas Traherne." *Bookman* (London), 82: 250.
480. "Thomas Traherne." *Contemporary Review*, 142: 386–388.
481. Wade, Gladys I., editor. Poetical Works of Thomas Traherne. A re-editing of Dobell's editions of 1903 and 1906, with the addition of 'Poems of Felicity.' 405 pp. London: Dobell.
482. Wilde, Hans O. "Thomas Traherne." Beiträge zur englischen Literaturgeschichte des 17 Jahrhunderts. 52 pp. Breslau.

1933

483. Winterbottom, K. M. Certain Affinities to Wordsworth in the Poetry of Vaughan and Traherne. Unpublished dissertation, University of Pittsburgh.

1934

484. Leishman, James B. The Metaphysical Poets: Donne, Herbert, Vaughan, Traherne. 239 pp. Oxford: Clarendon.

485. Quiller-Couch, Arthur, editor. The Felicities of Thomas Traherne. 144 pp. London: Dobell.

486. Wade, Gladys I. "Traherne and the Spiritual Value of Nature Study." *London Quarterly Review*, 159: 243–245.

487. Wade, Gladys I. "Thomas Traherne as Divine Philosopher." *Hibbert Journal*, 32: 400–408.

1935

488. Iredale, Q. Thomas Traherne. 87 pp. Oxford: Blackwell.

1936

489. Hobhouse, S. "A Poet's Resurrection." *Spectator*, 157: 804.

490. Wade, Gladys I. "Mrs. Susanna Hopton." *English Review*, 62: 41–47.

491. White, Helen C. The Metaphysical Poets: a Study in Religious Experience. 444 pp. New York: Macmillan.

HENRY VAUGHAN

1912

492. Guiney, Louise I. "Lovelace and Vaughan: A Speculation." *Catholic World*, 95: 646–655.

1914

493. Guiney, Louise I. "Milton and Vaughan." *Quarterly Review*, 220: 353–364.

494. Martin, L. C., editor. The Works of Henry Vaughan. Two volumes. Oxford: Clarendon.

495. Vaughan, Henry. Sacred Poems. With a memoir by H. F. Lyte. (Bohn's Popular Library: reprint, with slight changes, of Pickering edition of 1847.) 317 pp. New York: Macmillan; London: Bell.

1915

496. Guiney, Louise I. "Unpublished Letters, with a Commentary." *Nation* (New York), 100: 275–278, 300–303.
497. More, Paul Elmer. "Some Parallels in Henry Vaughan." *Nation* (New York), 101: 516–517.
498. "The Poetry of Henry Vaughan." *Living Age*, 286: 672–677.

1916

499. Brett-Smith, H. F. B. "Vaughan and D'Avenant." *Modern Language Review*, 11: 76–78.
500. Lyttleton, E. "Henry Vaughan and Optimism." *Contemporary Review*, 109: 462–469.
501. More, Paul Elmer. "Henry Vaughan." *Nation* (New York), 102: 247–250.

1918

502. Meynell, Francis, editor. The Best of Both Worlds. A choice taken from the poems of Andrew Marvell and Henry Vaughan. 60 pp. London: Allen and Unwin.

1919

503. Bensly, Edward. "Notes on Henry Vaughan." *Modern Language Review*, 14: 103–105.

1921

504. Clutton-Brock, Arthur. "Henry Vaughan." More Essays on Books. London: Methuen; New York: Dutton.

1922

505. Merrill, L. R. "Vaughan's Influence upon Wordsworth's Poetry." *Modern Language Notes*, 37: 91–96.

506. "The Tercentenary of Henry Vaughan." *Times Literary Supplement*, April 20, pages 249–250.

507. Wells, Henry W. The Tercentenary of Henry Vaughan. 16 pp. New York: Hudson Press.

1923

508. Loudon, M. K. Two Mystic Poets and Other Essays. 97 pp. Oxford: Blackwell.

509. Waite, A. E. "Henry and Thomas Vaughan." *Bookman* (London), 63: 240.

1924

510. George, Robert E. G. Outflying Philosophy . . . By Robert Sencourt (pseudonym). 358 pp. Hildesheim: F. Borgmeyer. (London: Simpkin Marshall, 1925.) [*See* No. 22.]

511. Vaughan, Henry. Poems of Henry Vaughan the Silurist. Poems from 'Poems,' 'Olor Iscanus,' 'Silex Scintillans,' 'Thalia Rediviva'; an essay from 'The Mount of Olives'; and two letters from manuscripts in the Bodleian Library. Limited edition. 164 pp. London: Nonesuch.

512. Vaughan, Henry. Poems. Edited by Ernest Rhys. 120 pp. Newtown, Montgomeryshire: The Gregynog Press.

1925

513. Martin, L. C. "A Forgotten Poet of the Seventeenth Century." *Essays and Studies of The English Association*, 11: 5–32.

514. [Sassoon, Siegfried], attributed author. "At the Grave of Henry Vaughan." *London Mercury*, 11: 352.

1926

515. Blunden, Edmund. "On the Poems of Henry Vaughan." *London Mercury*, 15: 59–75. (Reprinted in On the Poems of Henry Vaughan. London: Cobden-Sanderson, 1927.) [*See* No. 518.]

516. Judson, A. C. "Cornelius Agrippa and Henry Vaughan." *Modern Language Notes*, 41: 178–181.

517. Lucas, F. L. "Henry Vaughan." Authors Dead and Living, pages 62–67. London: Chatto and Windus.

1927

518. Blunden, Edmund. On the Poems of Henry Vaughan: Characteristics and Intimations. With his principal Latin poems translated into English verse. 64 pp. London: Cobden-Sanderson. [*See* No. 515.]

519. Eliot, T. S. "The Silurist." *Dial*, 83: 259–263.

520. Judson, A. C. "Henry Vaughan as a Nature Poet." *Modern Language Association Publications*, 42: 146–156.

521. Martin, L. C. "Vaughan and Cowper." *Modern Language Review*, 22: 79–84.

1928

522. Vaughan, Henry. Three Poems—'Peace,' 'The Retreate,' 'Into the World of Light.' 8 pp. Washington: St. Albans Press.

523. More, Paul Elmer. "Henry Vaughan." The Demon of the Absolute, pages 143–164. (New Shelburne Essays, Volume One.) Princeton: University Press; London: Milford.

1929

524. Empson, William. "Henry Vaughan, Early Romantic." *Cambridge Review*, 50: 495–496.

1930

525. Collard, Lorna. "Henry Vaughan and the Region Elenore." *Occult Review*, 52: 299–308.

1932

526. Holmes, Elizabeth. Henry Vaughan and the Hermetic Philosophy. 71 pp. Blackwell.

527. Morgan, Gwenllian E. F. "Henry Vaughan, Oxford Silurist." *Times Literary Supplement*, November 2, page 815.

1933

528. Chapin, C. "Henry Vaughan and the Modern Spirit." *Nineteenth Century*, 114: 619–628.

529. Clough, W. O. "Henry Vaughan and the Hermetic Philosophy." *Modern Language Association Publications*, 48: 1108–1130.

530. Martin, Burns. "Vaughan's 'The World.'" *Times Literary Supplement*, August 3, page 525.

531. Smith, Arthur J. M. "Some Relations between Henry Vaughan and Thomas Vaughan." *Papers of the Michigan Academy of Sciences, Arts, and Letters*, 18: 551–561.

532. Winterbottom, K. M. Certain Affinities to Wordsworth in the Poetry of Vaughan and Traherne. Unpublished dissertation, University of Pittsburgh.

1934

533. Bennett, Joan. Four Metaphysical Poets: Donne, Herbert, Vaughan, and Crashaw. 135 pp. Cambridge: University Press.

534. Leishman, James B. The Metaphysical Poets: Donne, Herbert, Vaughan, Traherne. 239 pp. Oxford: Clarendon.

535. McMaster, Helen. "Wordsworth's Copy of Vaughan." *Times Literary Supplement*, April 12, page 262.

1935

536. McMaster, Helen. "Vaughan and Wordsworth." *Review of English Studies*, 11: 313–325.

1936

537. Wardle, Ralph M. "Thomas Vaughan's Influence upon the Poetry of Henry Vaughan." *Modern Language Association Publications*, 51: 936–952.

. 538. White, Helen C. The Metaphysical Poets: a Study in Religious Experience. 444 pp. New York: Macmillan.

1937

539. Vaughan, Henry. A Few Lines by a Welsh Doctor. 7 pp. New York: Oliver.

1938

540. Martin, L. C. "Henry Vaughan and The Theme of Infancy." Seventeenth Century Studies Presented to Sir Herbert Grierson, pages 243–255. Oxford: Clarendon.

Index to Bibliography